AMAZING ACTIVIT...

Arvind Gupta graduated from the Indian Institute of Technology, Kanpur in 1975 with a degree in Electrical Engineering. He has written 15 science activity books, translated 140 books into Hindi and presented 125 films on science activities on Doordarshan. His first book *Matchstick Models & Other Science Experiments* was translated into 12 Indian languages and sold over half a million copies. He has received several honours, including the inaugural National Award for Science Popularization amongst Children (1988), the Distinguished Alumnus Award of IIT Kanpur (2000), the Indira Gandhi Award for Science Popularization (2008) and the Third World Academy of Science Award (2010) for making science interesting for children. Currently he works at IUCAA's Children's Science Centre, Pune, and shares his passion for books and toys through his popular website http://arvindguptatoys.com

Reshma Barve studied Commercial Art at the Abhinav Kala Mahavidyalaya, Pune. She is a freelance artist and designer and has illustrated many children's books.

AMAZING ACTIVITIES

ARVIND GUPTA

ILLUSTRATIONS BY
RESHMA BARVE

SCHOLASTIC
New York Toronto London Auckland
Sydney New Delhi Hong Kong

Dedicated to Mr. K. V. Potdar,
our mentor and guide who generously
shared many of these activities with us.

This book was developed under a grant from the Navajibai Ratan Tata Trust.

Published by Scholastic India Pvt. Ltd.
A subsidiary of Scholastic Inc., New York, 10012 (USA).
Publishers since 1920, with international operations in Canada, Australia, New Zealand, the United Kingdom, India, and Hong Kong.

First edition: May 2012

ISBN-13: 978-81-8477-859-5

Activities

AREA OF A TRIANGLE

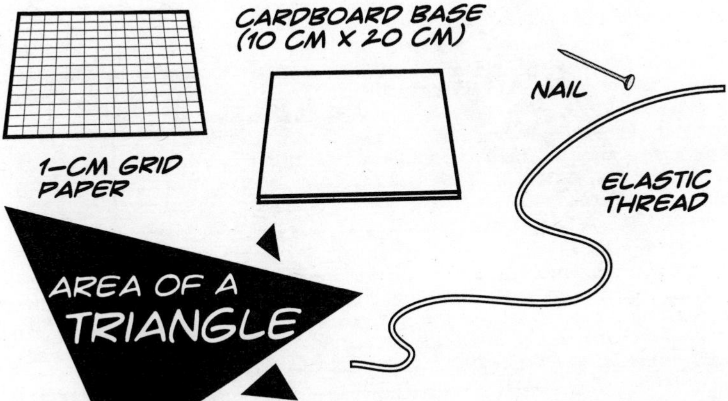

1. MAKE HOLES ON TOP NODES.

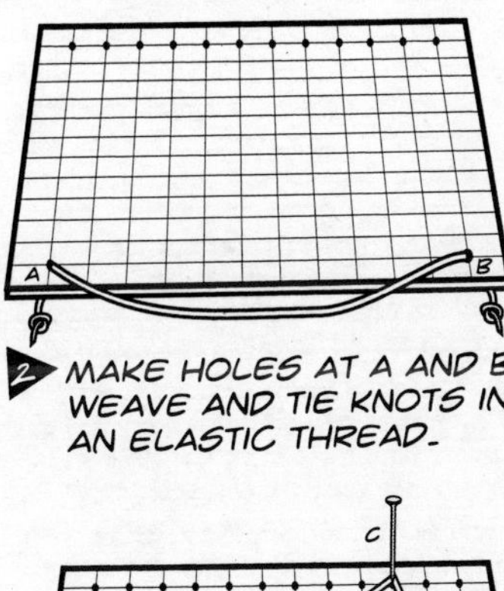

2. MAKE HOLES AT A AND B. WEAVE AND TIE KNOTS IN AN ELASTIC THREAD.

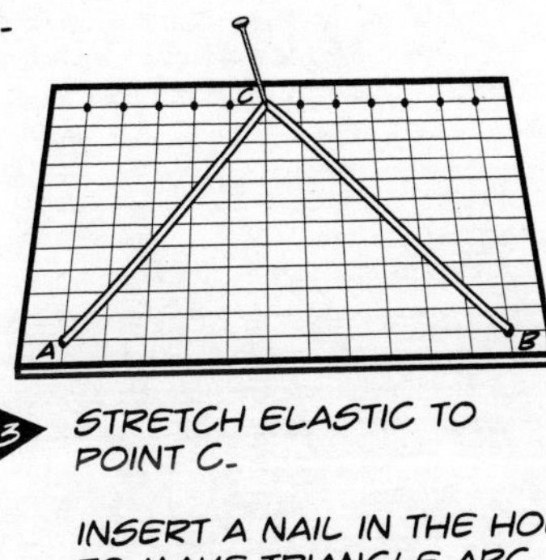

3. STRETCH ELASTIC TO POINT C.

INSERT A NAIL IN THE HOLE TO MAKE TRIANGLE ABC.

COUNT SQUARES IN THE TRIANGLE TO ESTIMATE ITS AREA.

IGNORE LESS-THAN-HALF SQUARES. COUNT MORE-THAN-HALF SQUARES AS ONE.

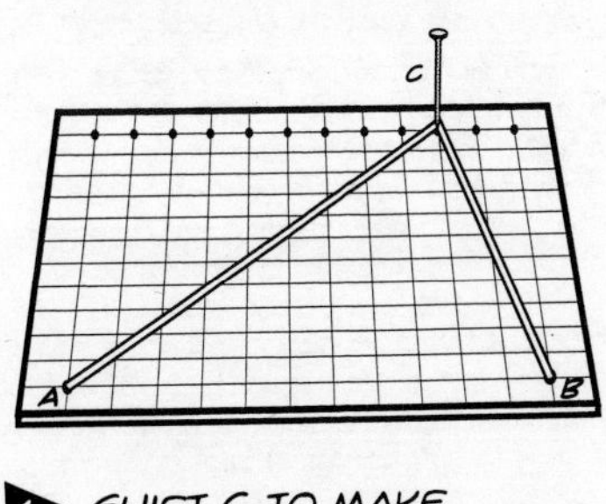

4. SHIFT C TO MAKE YET ANOTHER TRIANGLE AND MEASURE ITS AREA.

5. ALL THESE TRIANGLES WILL HAVE THE SAME BASE AND HEIGHT, SO THEY WILL ENCLOSE THE SAME AREA.

TILT BALANCE

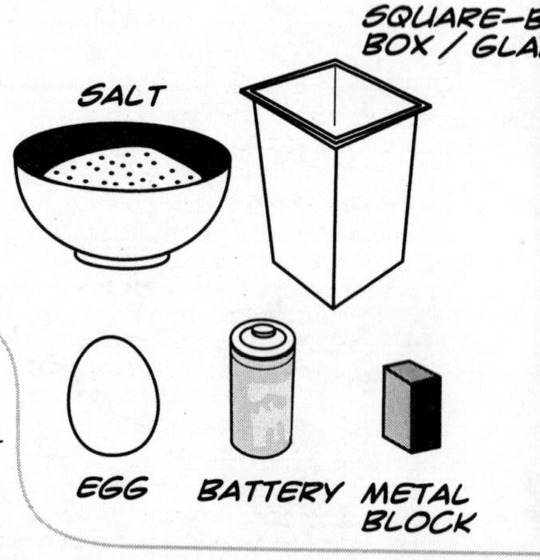

1. PLACE A PINCH OF SALT ON THE TABLE.

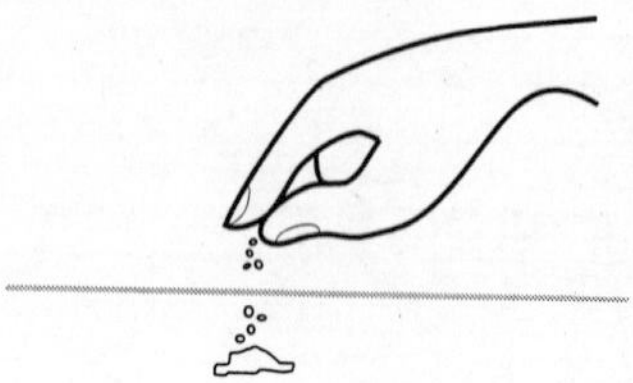

2. TRY MAKING THE EGG STAND ON A FEW GRAINS OF SALT. DON'T GIVE UP. YOU WILL SUCCEED!

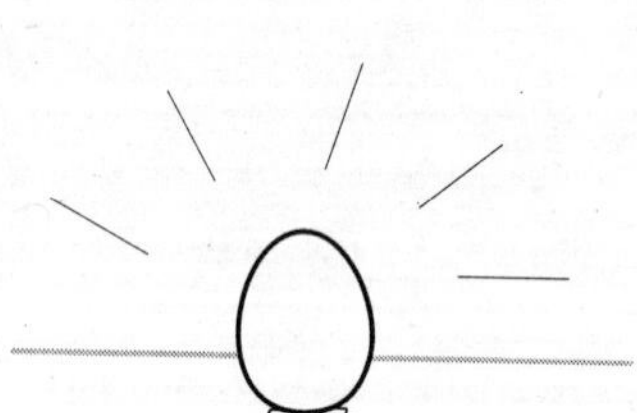

3. SIMILARLY, MAKE ONE EDGE OF A METAL BLOCK OR A SQUARE GLASS STAND ON A FEW GRAINS OF SALT.

4. NOW TRY RECLINING A BATTERY ON A FEW GRAINS OF SALT.

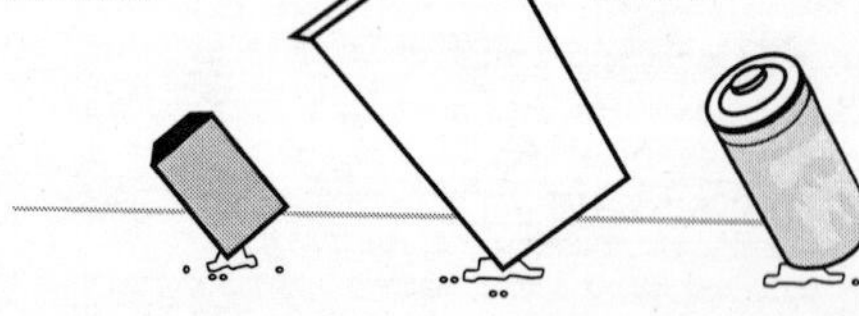

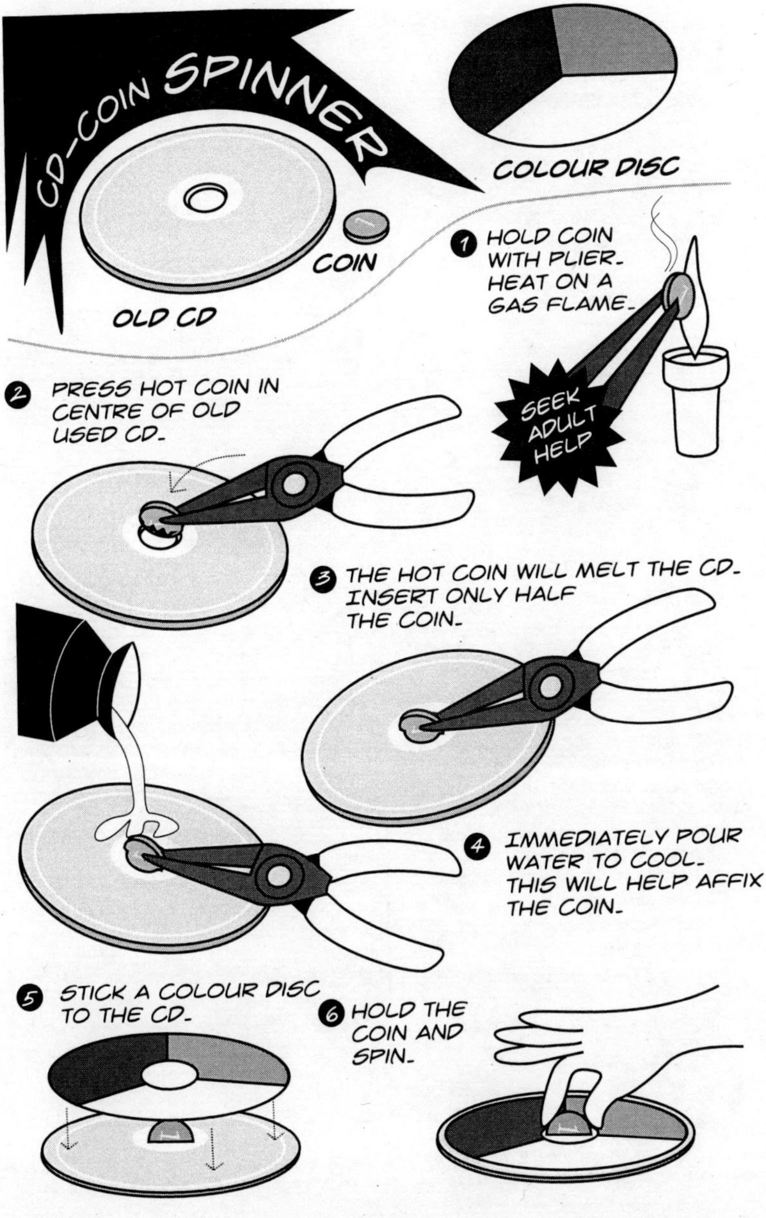
CD-COIN SPINNER
COLOUR DISC
OLD CD
COIN
1 HOLD COIN WITH PLIER. HEAT ON A GAS FLAME.
SEEK ADULT HELP
2 PRESS HOT COIN IN CENTRE OF OLD USED CD.
3 THE HOT COIN WILL MELT THE CD. INSERT ONLY HALF THE COIN.
4 IMMEDIATELY POUR WATER TO COOL. THIS WILL HELP AFFIX THE COIN.
5 STICK A COLOUR DISC TO THE CD.
6 HOLD THE COIN AND SPIN.

SIMPLE TESSELLATION

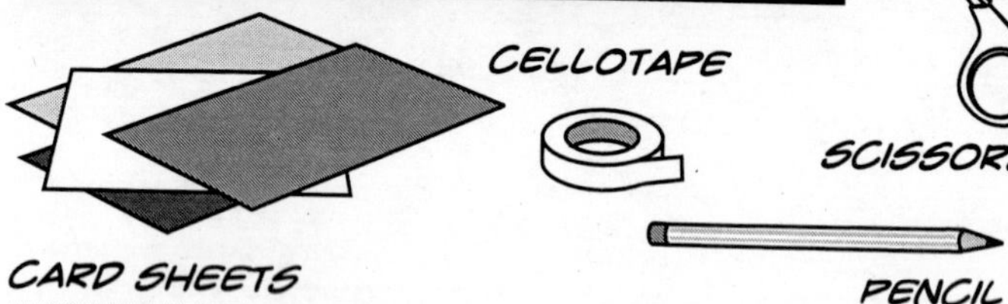

1. CUT A 10–CM SQUARE FROM A CARD SHEET.

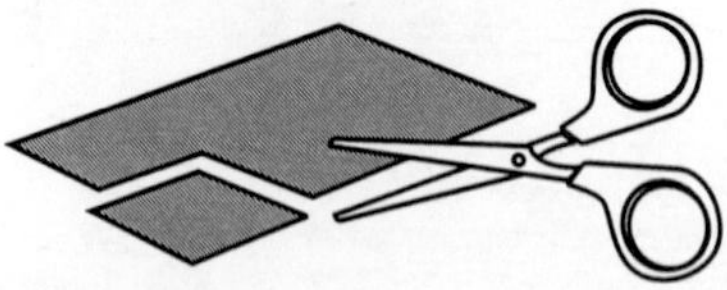

2. DRAW TRIANGLES THE WAY IT HAS BEEN SHOWN.

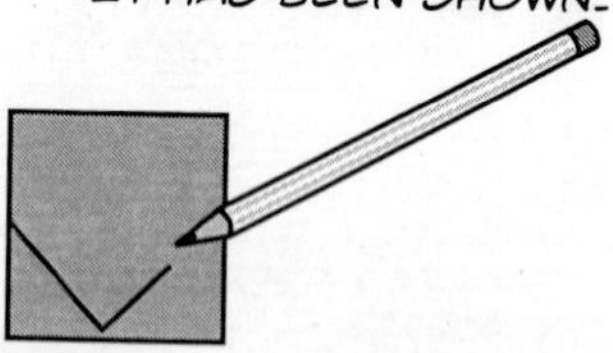

3. CUT TRIANGLES.

4. SHIFT TRIANGLES.

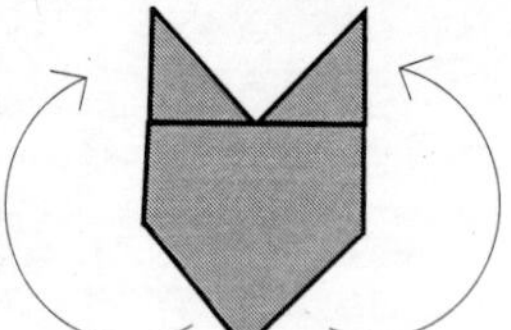

5. SECURE TRIANGLES WITH TAPE.

6. CUT OUT A BEAK AND STICK IT WITH TAPE.

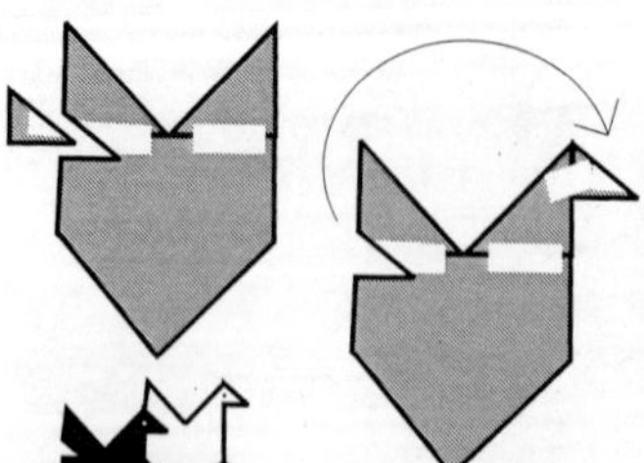

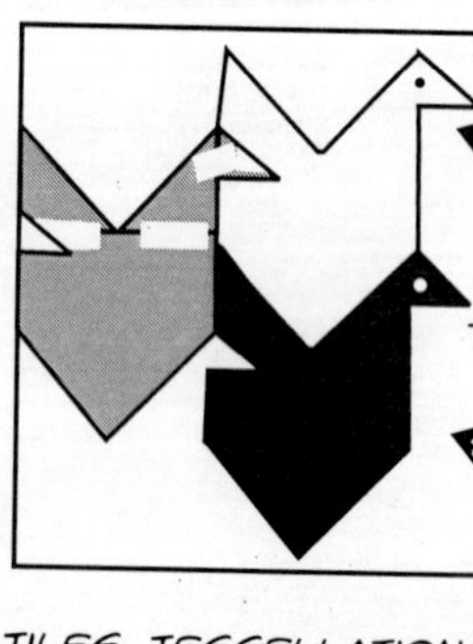

7. MAKE MANY BIRDS USING THIS TEMPLATE.

8. DRAW THEIR EYES.

LIKE FLOOR TILES, TESSELLATIONS ALSO USE THE SAME PATTERN TO COVER AN AREA.

TUG OF WAR

2 SIMILAR BOOKS

1. TAKE TWO BOOKS OF THE SAME SIZE.

2. PUT THE BACK COVER OF BOOK 1 ON THE FRONT COVER OF BOOK 2.

3. ALTERNATIVELY, PLACE PAGES OF BOOK 1 ON THE PAGES OF BOOK 2.

4. THE PAGES OF THE TWO BOOKS WILL BE INTERLOCKED.

FINALLY, THE BOOKS WILL LOOK LIKE THIS.

5. NOW IF YOU HOLD THE BOOKS ON THEIR SEAMS AND PULL OUT, YOU WILL FAIL!

FISHY FISH

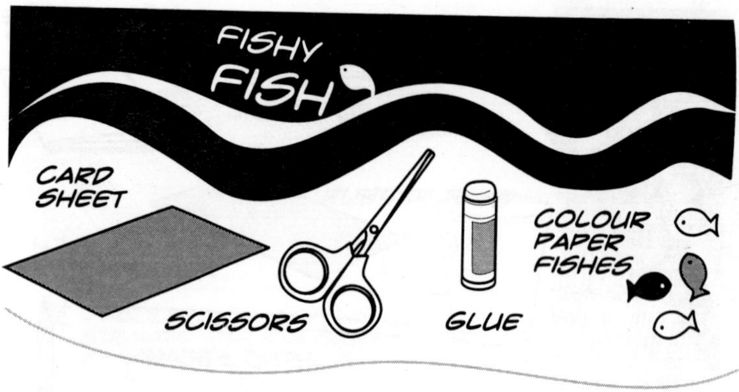

1. FOLD THE CARD SHEET IN HALF.

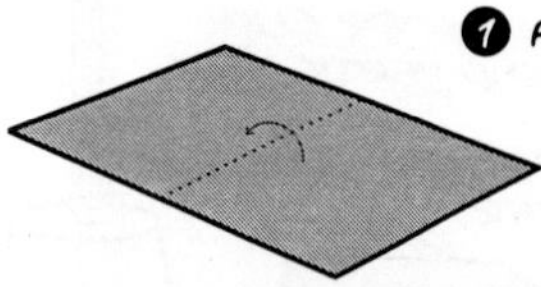

2. CUT SEVERAL WAVY LINES AWAY FROM THE FOLD.

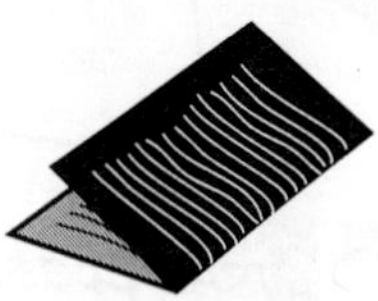

3. LEAVE 1–CM UNCUT FROM THE EDGES.

THE CUT LINES WILL MAKE SEA WAVES.

4. FOLD ALTERNATE STRIPS BACK AND PINCH.

THE STRIPS WILL LOOK LIKE SEA WAVES.

3. STICK COLOUR FISHES ON THE WAVES. THE FISHES WILL APPEAR TO BE SWIMMING IN THE SEA.

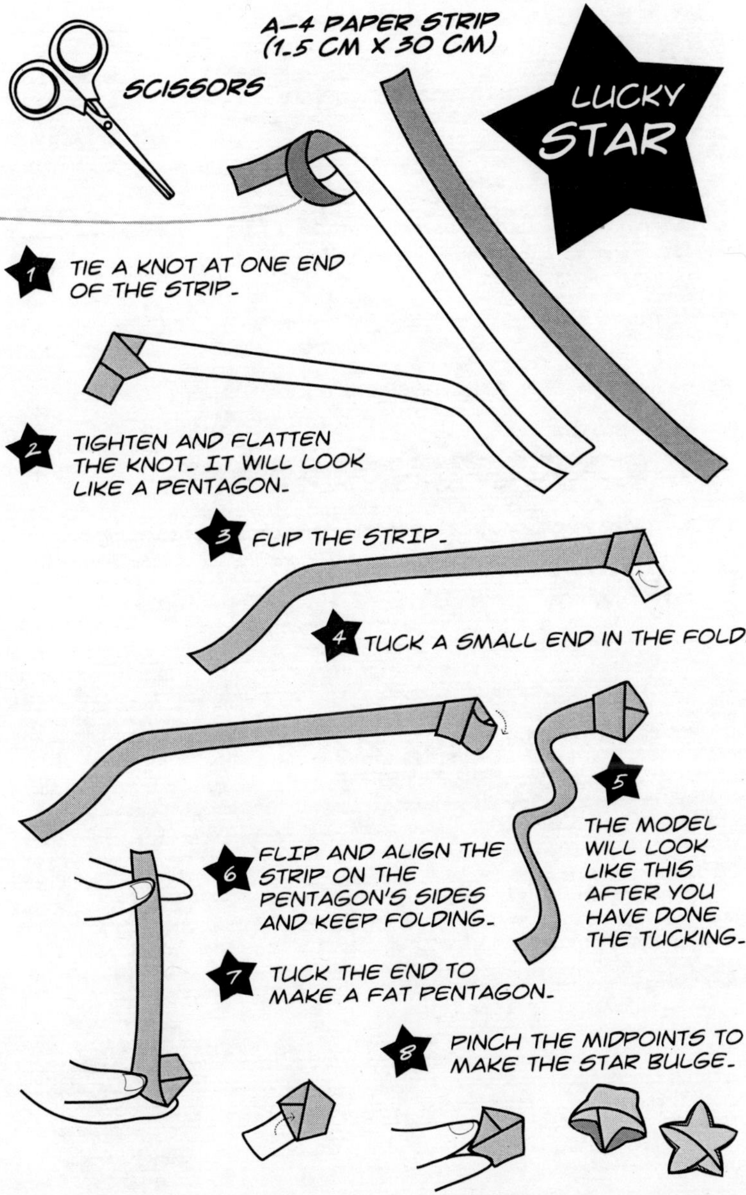
LUCKY STAR
SCISSORS
A-4 PAPER STRIP (1.5 CM X 30 CM)
1 TIE A KNOT AT ONE END OF THE STRIP.
2 TIGHTEN AND FLATTEN THE KNOT. IT WILL LOOK LIKE A PENTAGON.
3 FLIP THE STRIP.
4 TUCK A SMALL END IN THE FOLD.
5 THE MODEL WILL LOOK LIKE THIS AFTER YOU HAVE DONE THE TUCKING.
6 FLIP AND ALIGN THE STRIP ON THE PENTAGON'S SIDES AND KEEP FOLDING.
7 TUCK THE END TO MAKE A FAT PENTAGON.
8 PINCH THE MIDPOINTS TO MAKE THE STAR BULGE.

PAPER WAVES

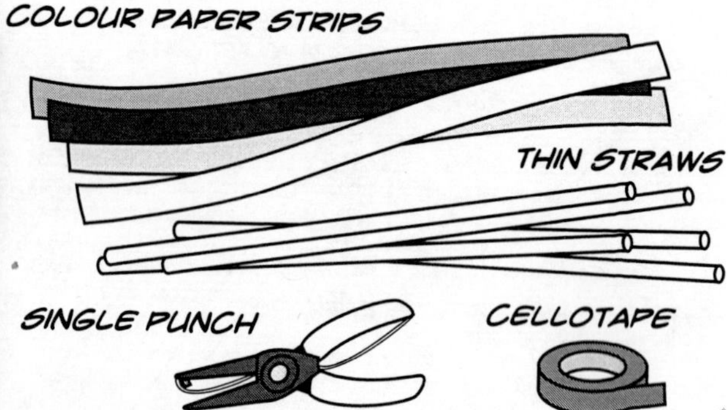

1 FANFOLD A COLOUR PAPER STRIP.

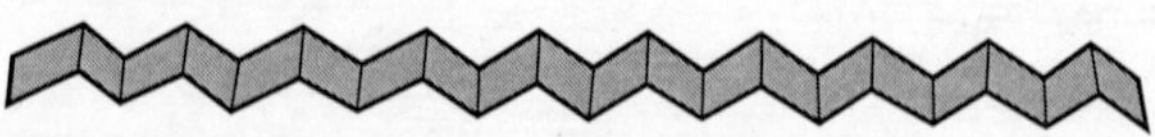

2 COMPRESS ITS FOLDS.

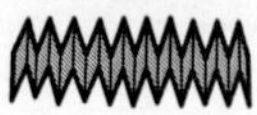

3 MAKE A THROUGH HOLE WITH A SINGLE PUNCH.

4 OPEN FOLDS LIKE AN ACCORDION.

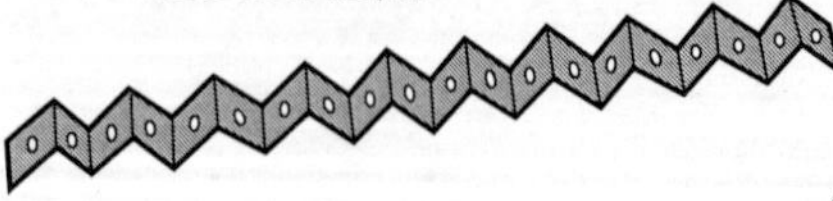

5 THEN WEAVE A STRAW IN THROUGH THE HOLES OF THE WAVY STRIP.

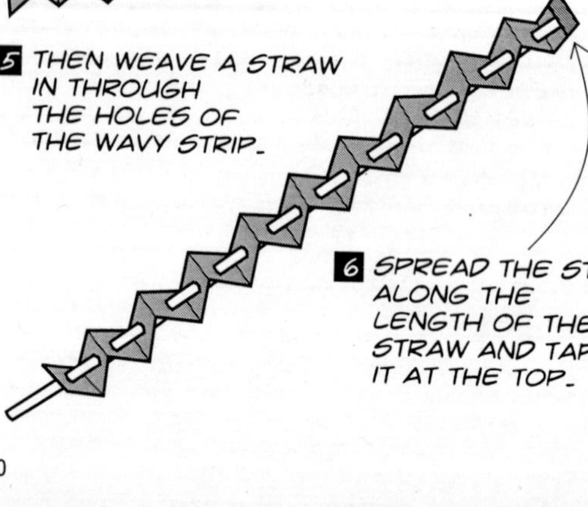

6 SPREAD THE STRIP ALONG THE LENGTH OF THE STRAW AND TAPE IT AT THE TOP.

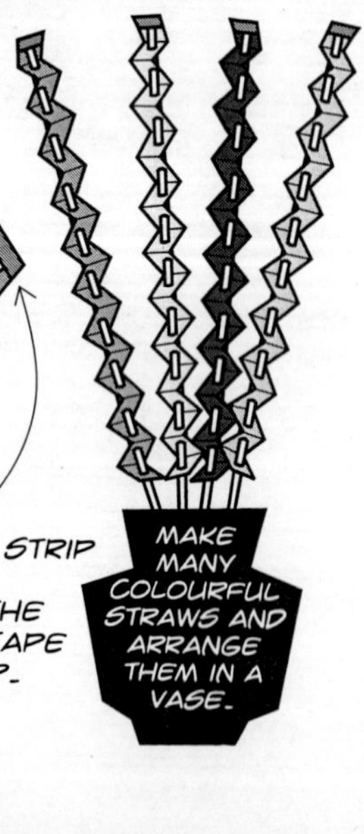

STRIP TETRA

CELLOTAPE

PAPER STRIP (28 CM X 4 CM)

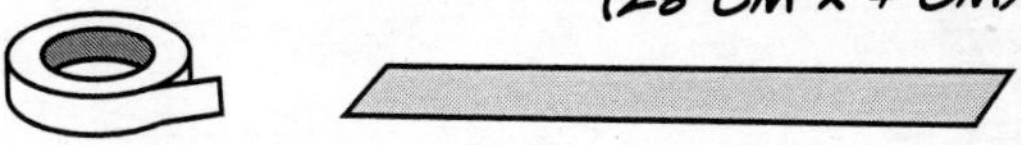

1 FOLD A 28-CM X 4-CM PAPER STRIP IN HALF. BRING THE FREE ENDS TOGETHER ...

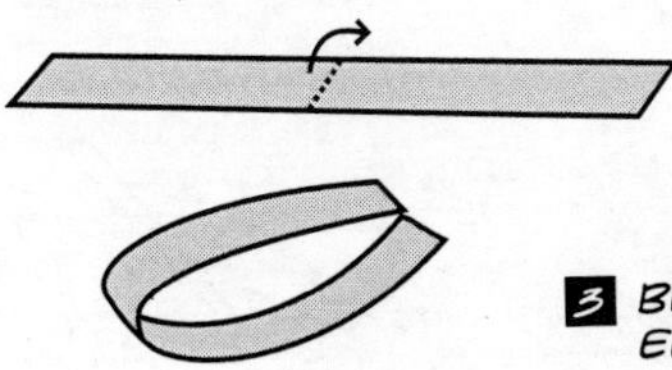

2 ... AND TAPE THEM.

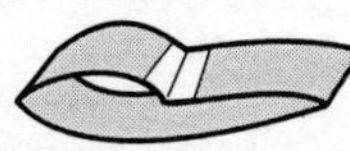

3 BRING THE TAPED END TO ONE SIDE.

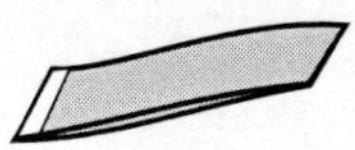

4 FOLD AGAIN IN HALF.

5 MAKE MOUNTAIN/VALLEY FOLDS ALONG DIAGONALS. OPEN THE MODEL.

6 OPEN UP LIKE A BOAT. BRING THE TWO EDGES TOGETHER ...

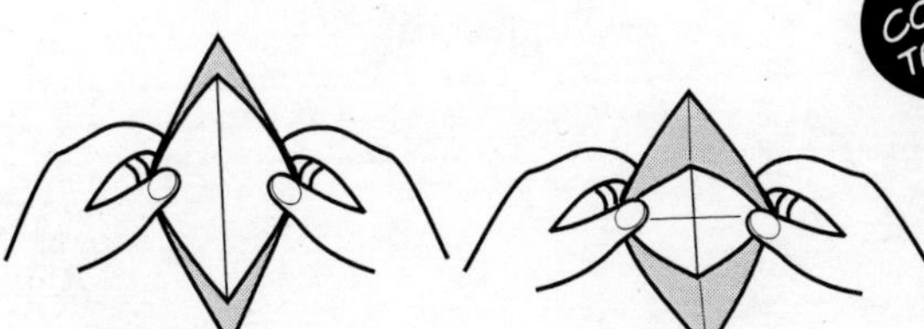

... TO COMPLETE THE TETRAHEDRON!

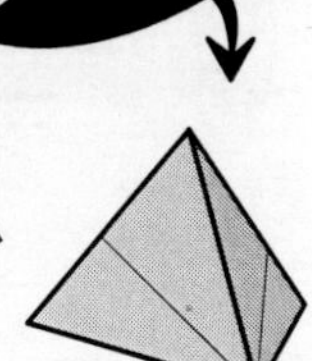

ENVELOPE PETALS

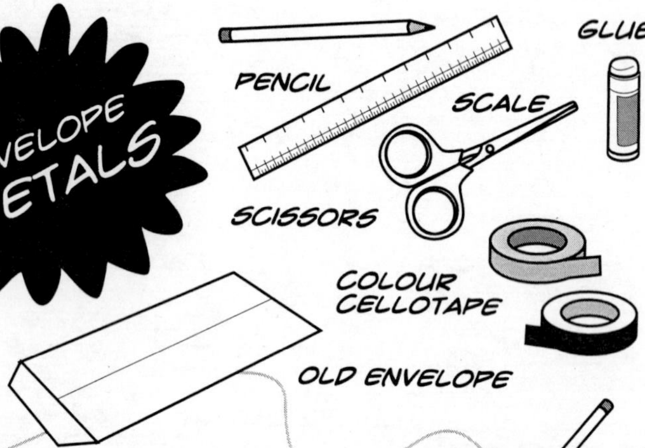

1. DRAW PARALLEL LINES 1 CM BELOW THE TOP EDGE OF AN OLD ENVELOPE.

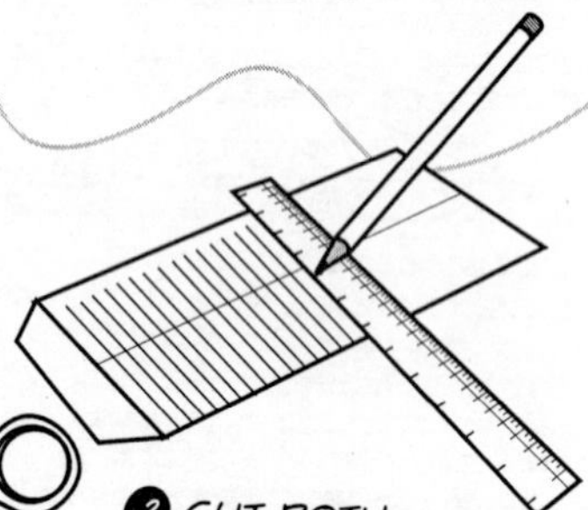

2. CUT BOTH ENDS OF THE ENVELOPE.

3. STICK COLOUR TAPE ON THE ENVELOPE AND CUT ALONG THE MARKED LINES.

4. OPEN THE PETALS WITH BOTH HANDS TO MAKE A CIRCULAR FLOWER AND TAPE BOTH ENDS.

PAPER CHANDELIER

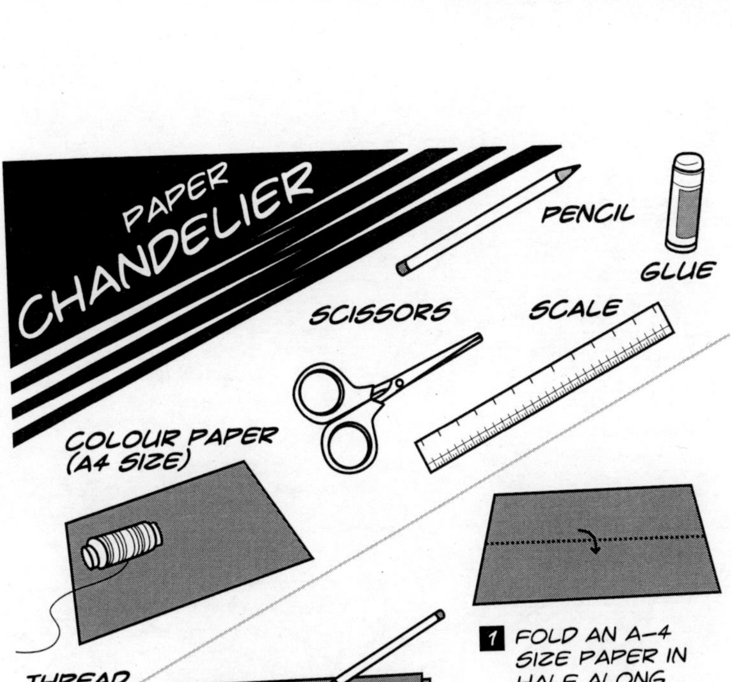

1 FOLD AN A-4 SIZE PAPER IN HALF ALONG ITS WIDTH.

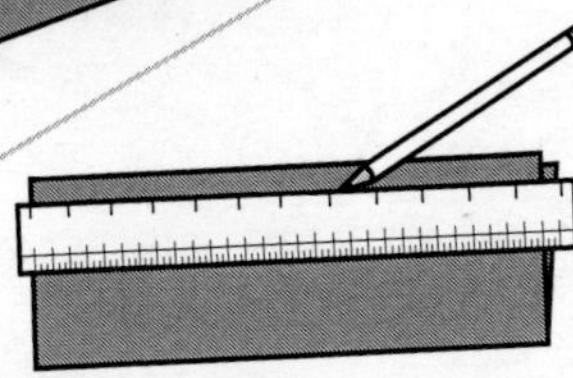

2 MARK A 1-CM MARGIN ALONG THE OPEN ENDS.

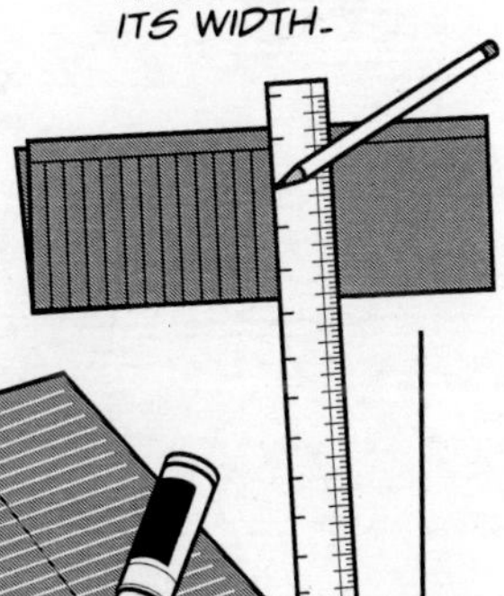

3 DRAW 1-CM-WIDE PARALLEL LINES ALL ALONG THE LENGTH OF THE PAPER AND CUT THIN STRIPS.

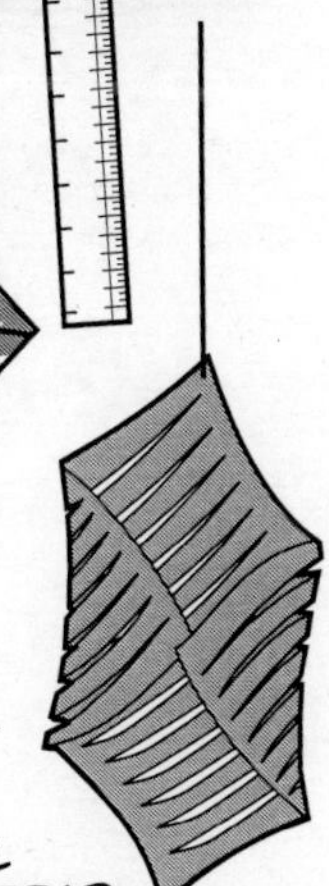

4 OPEN FULLY AND STICK THE OPPOSITE CORNERS WITH GLUE.

5 HANG THIS BEAUTIFUL CHANDELIER BY A THREAD.

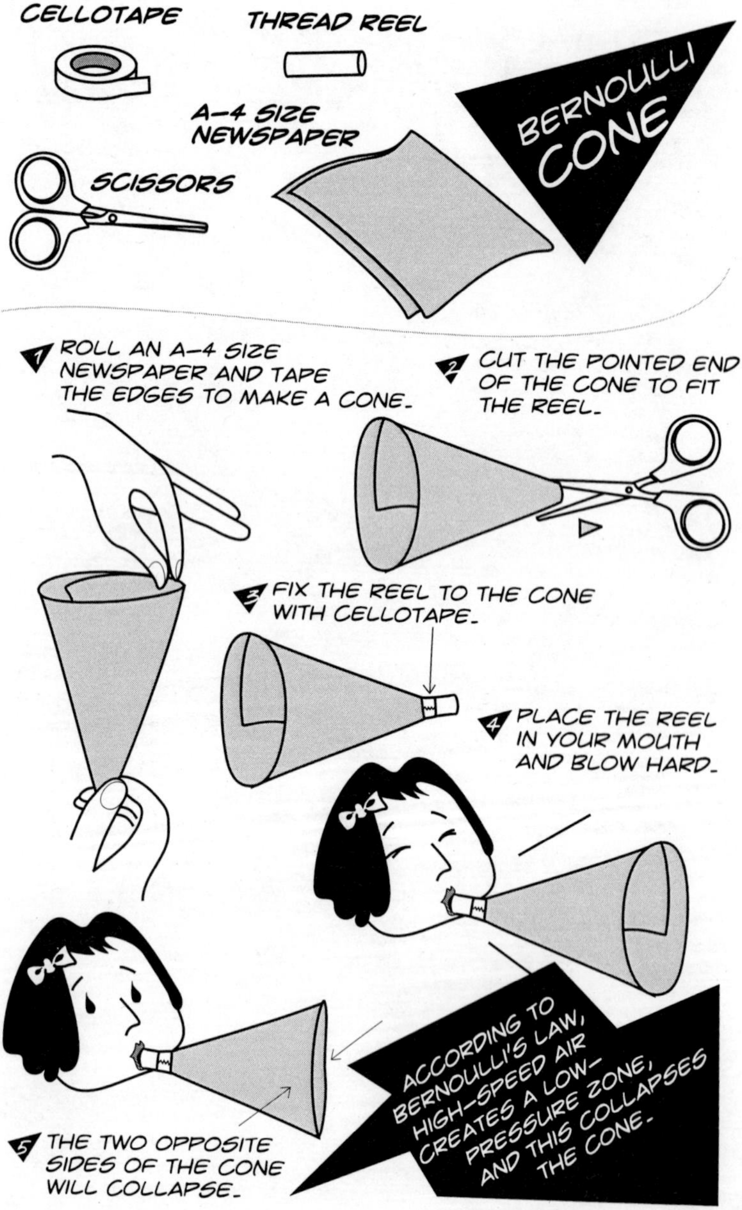
BERNOULLI CONE
CELLOTAPE
THREAD REEL
A-4 SIZE NEWSPAPER
SCISSORS
1 ROLL AN A-4 SIZE NEWSPAPER AND TAPE THE EDGES TO MAKE A CONE.
2 CUT THE POINTED END OF THE CONE TO FIT THE REEL.
3 FIX THE REEL TO THE CONE WITH CELLOTAPE.
4 PLACE THE REEL IN YOUR MOUTH AND BLOW HARD.
5 THE TWO OPPOSITE SIDES OF THE CONE WILL COLLAPSE.
ACCORDING TO BERNOULLI'S LAW, HIGH-SPEED AIR CREATES A LOW-PRESSURE ZONE, AND THIS COLLAPSES THE CONE.

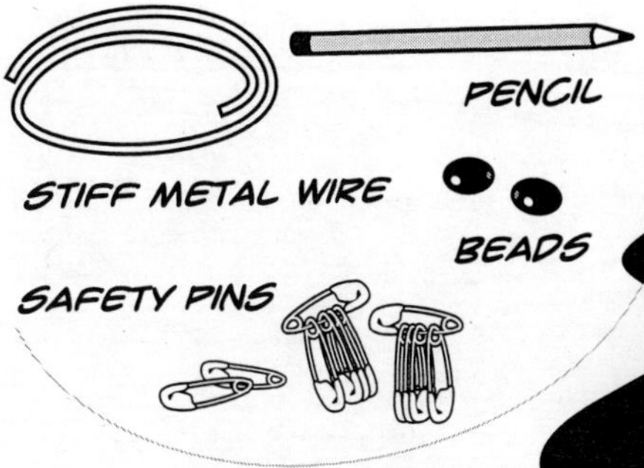

1. WIND A 60-CM-LONG WIRE ON A PENCIL TO MAKE A SPRING.

2. REMOVE THE SPRING FROM THE PENCIL.

3. PULL THE ENDS OF THE SPRING TO MAKE A SPIRAL.

4. WEAVE A DOZEN SAFETY PINS.

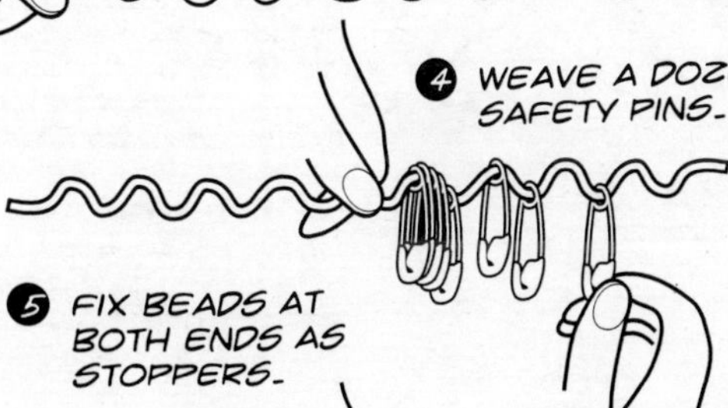

5. FIX BEADS AT BOTH ENDS AS STOPPERS.

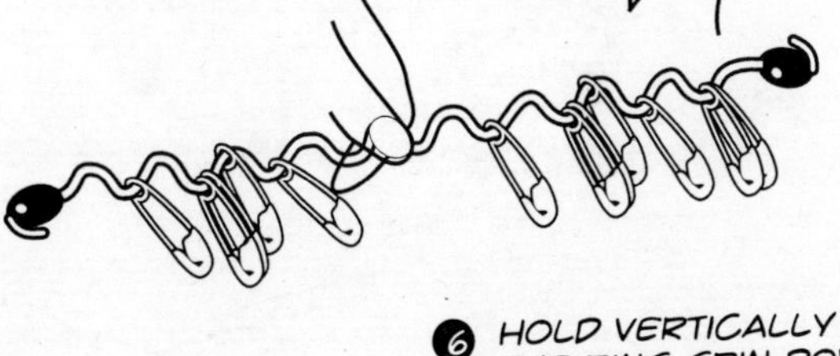

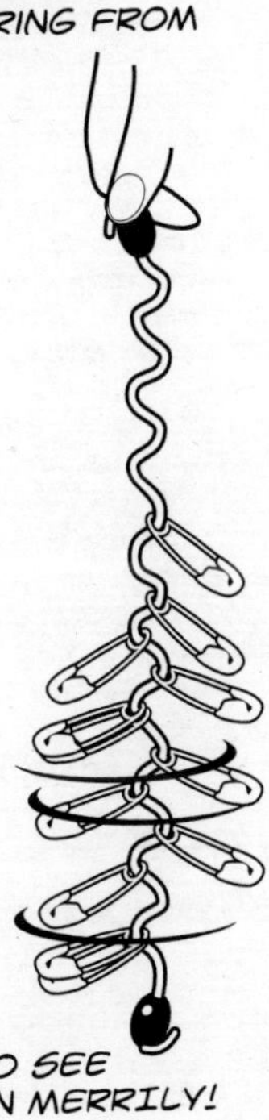

6. HOLD VERTICALLY TO SEE THE PINS SPIN DOWN MERRILY!

MOVING MONKEY

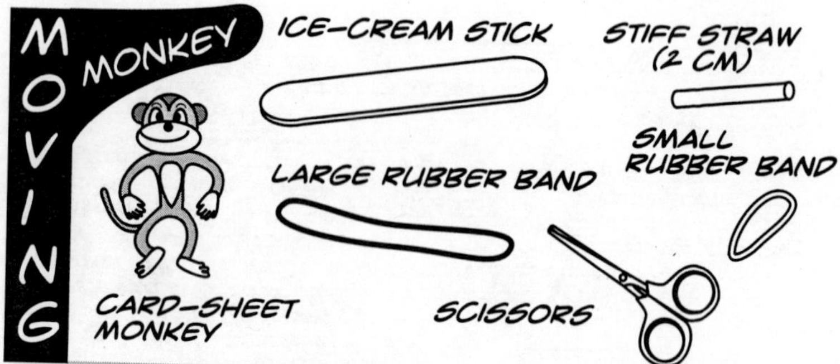

1. FIX A 2-CM STIFF STRAW TO AN ICE-CREAM STICK WITH A SMALL RUBBER BAND.

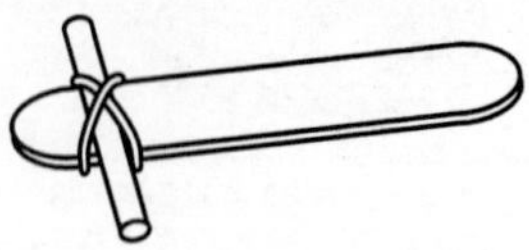

2. CUT A LARGE RUBBER BAND.

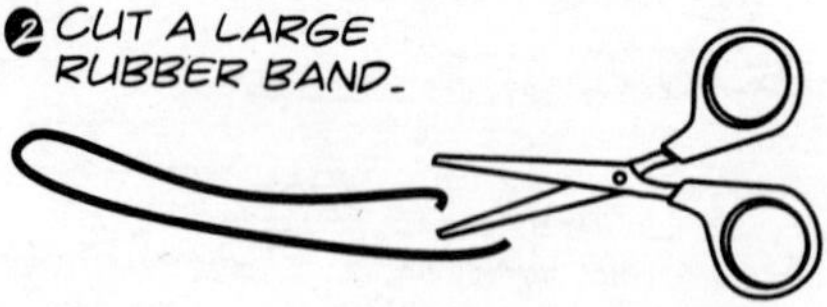

3. WEAVE IT THROUGH THE STRAW AS SHOWN. TIE KNOTS AT BOTH ENDS.

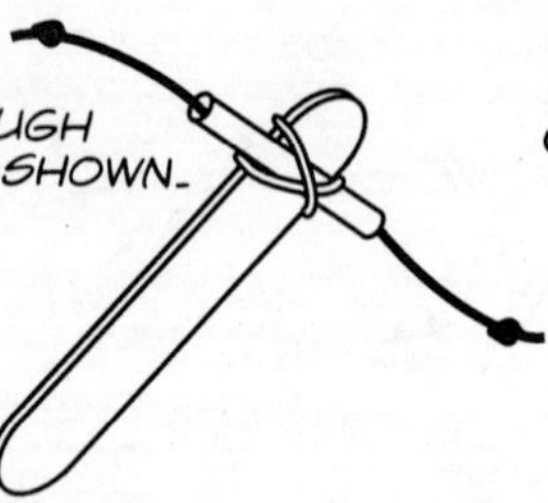

4. FIX THE CARD-SHEET MONKEY ON THE STICK.

5. ON STRETCHING THE RUBBER BAND THE MONKEY WILL FALL IN SHORT JERKS.

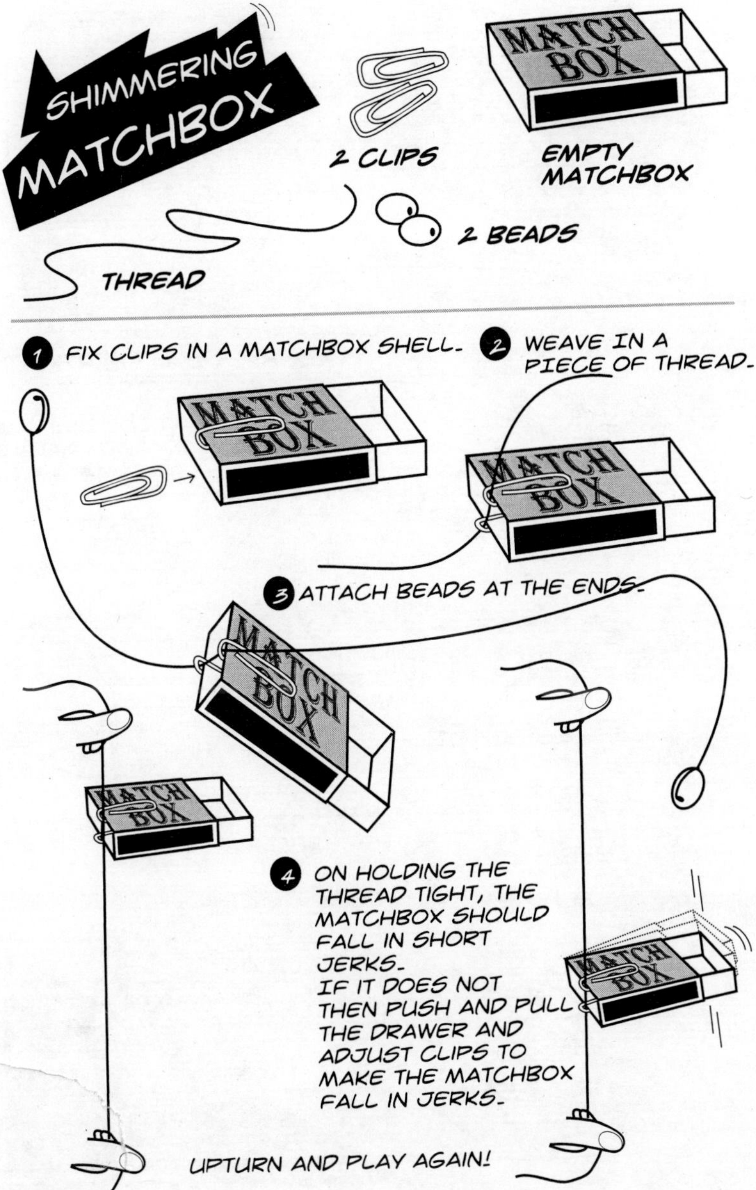
SHIMMERING MATCHBOX
2 CLIPS
MATCH BOX
EMPTY MATCHBOX
2 BEADS
THREAD
1 FIX CLIPS IN A MATCHBOX SHELL.
2 WEAVE IN A PIECE OF THREAD.
3 ATTACH BEADS AT THE ENDS.
4 ON HOLDING THE THREAD TIGHT, THE MATCHBOX SHOULD FALL IN SHORT JERKS.
IF IT DOES NOT THEN PUSH AND PULL THE DRAWER AND ADJUST CLIPS TO MAKE THE MATCHBOX FALL IN JERKS.
UPTURN AND PLAY AGAIN!

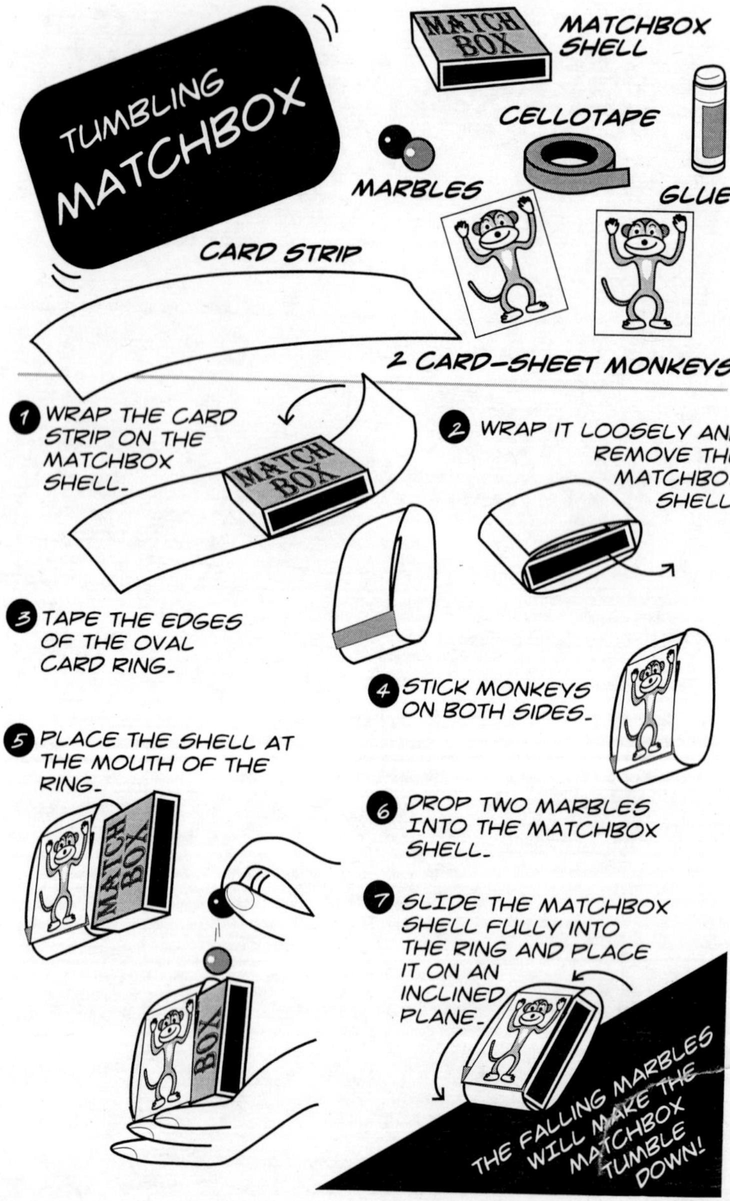
TUMBLING MATCHBOX
MATCHBOX SHELL
CELLOTAPE
MARBLES
GLUE
CARD STRIP
2 CARD-SHEET MONKEYS
1 WRAP THE CARD STRIP ON THE MATCHBOX SHELL.
2 WRAP IT LOOSELY AND REMOVE THE MATCHBOX SHELL.
3 TAPE THE EDGES OF THE OVAL CARD RING.
4 STICK MONKEYS ON BOTH SIDES.
5 PLACE THE SHELL AT THE MOUTH OF THE RING.
6 DROP TWO MARBLES INTO THE MATCHBOX SHELL.
7 SLIDE THE MATCHBOX SHELL FULLY INTO THE RING AND PLACE IT ON AN INCLINED PLANE.
THE FALLING MARBLES WILL MAKE THE MATCHBOX TUMBLE DOWN!

MOTHER AND CHILD

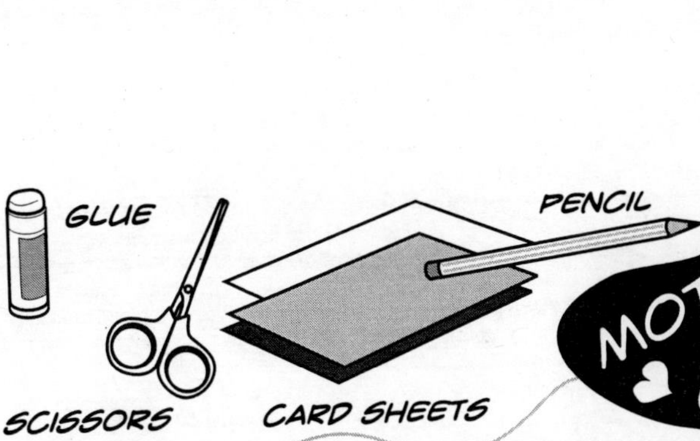

1. DRAW A MOTHER AND CHILD.

2. CUT BOTH PICTURES ALONG THEIR OUTLINES.

3. APPLY GLUE ON BOTH HANDS OF THE MOTHER.

4. STICK THE MOTHER'S HANDS AT THE CHILD'S WAIST, SO THAT IT LOOKS LIKE THE MOTHER IS HOLDING THE CHILD UP.

5. STICK THE MOTHER AND CHILD ON THE DARK CARD SHEET.

6. NOW USE THIS WALL HANGING TO DECORATE YOUR ROOM!

JET CAR

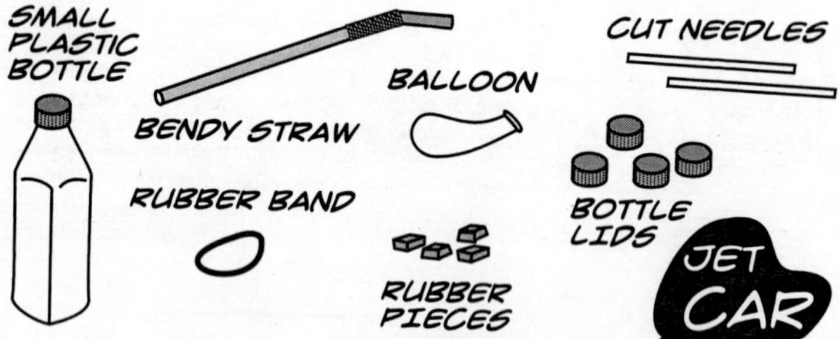

1. MAKE FOUR HOLES IN A BOTTLE. WEAVE CUT NEEDLES THROUGH THEM TO MAKE WHEEL AXLES.

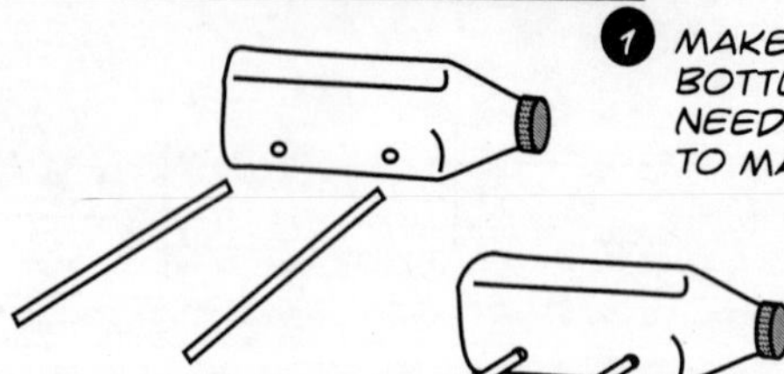

2. MAKE HOLES IN BOTTLE LIDS TO MAKE WHEELS.

3. MAKE TWO HOLES IN THE BOTTLE, ONE AT THE BASE AND THE OTHER AT THE TOP.

4. ATTACH A BALLOON TO THE STRAW WITH A RUBBER BAND.

5. INFLATE THE BALLOON AND CLOSE THE MOUTH OF THE STRAW WITH YOUR THUMB.

6. WHEN YOU PLACE IT ON A SMOOTH FLOOR THE CAR WILL SHOOT FORWARD!

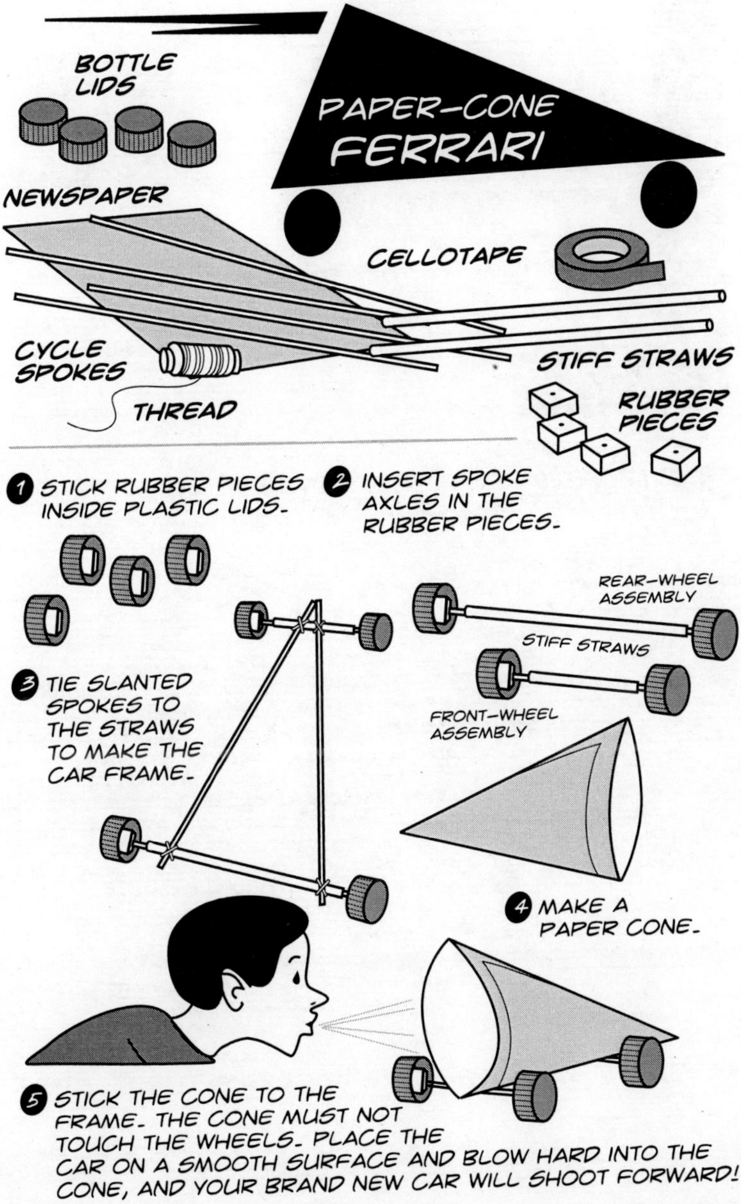
PAPER-CONE FERRARI
BOTTLE LIDS
NEWSPAPER
CELLOTAPE
CYCLE SPOKES
THREAD
STIFF STRAWS
RUBBER PIECES
1 STICK RUBBER PIECES INSIDE PLASTIC LIDS.
2 INSERT SPOKE AXLES IN THE RUBBER PIECES.
REAR-WHEEL ASSEMBLY
STIFF STRAWS
FRONT-WHEEL ASSEMBLY
3 TIE SLANTED SPOKES TO THE STRAWS TO MAKE THE CAR FRAME.
4 MAKE A PAPER CONE.
5 STICK THE CONE TO THE FRAME. THE CONE MUST NOT TOUCH THE WHEELS. PLACE THE CAR ON A SMOOTH SURFACE AND BLOW HARD INTO THE CONE, AND YOUR BRAND NEW CAR WILL SHOOT FORWARD!

TRAFFIC POLICE

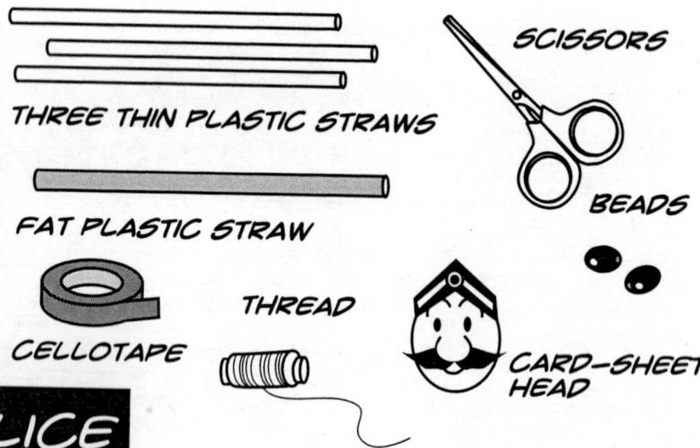

1. CUT FOUR 'V' NOTCHES IN TWO THIN STRAWS. THE NOTCHES SHOULD BE 3 CM APART.

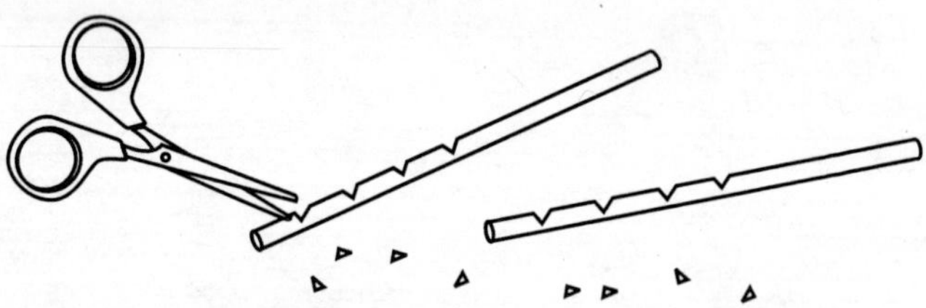

2. WEAVE A THIN THREAD THROUGH BOTH THE STRAWS.

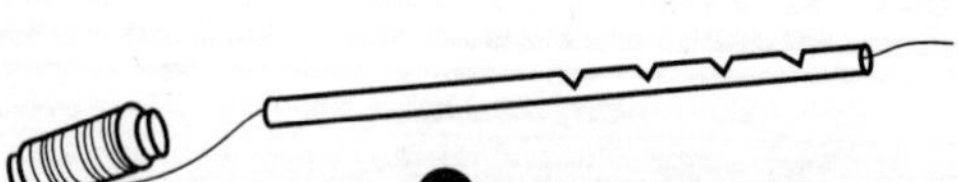

3. TAPE ONE END OF EACH PIECE OF THREAD WITH THE STRAWS.

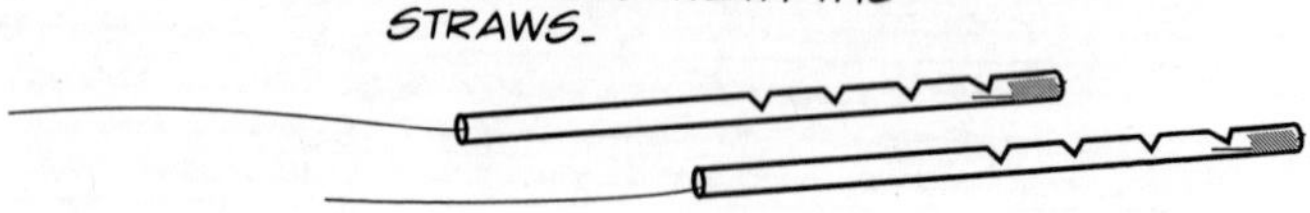

4. PLACE BOTH THIN STRAWS WITH THREADS INSIDE A FAT STRAW.

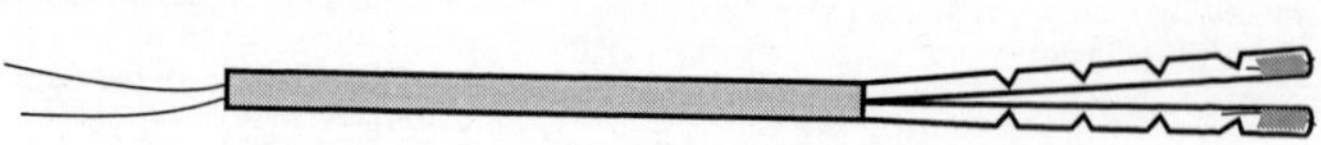

BOBBING BUTTERFLY

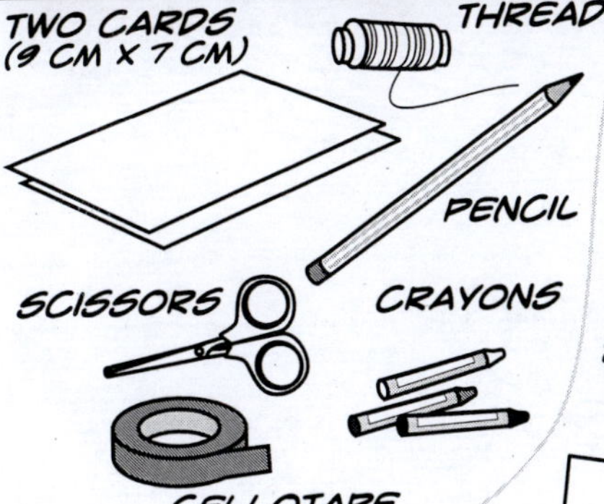

1. MAKE HALF CUTS IN BOTH CARDS.

2. INTERLOCK CUTS TO MAKE AN 'X'.

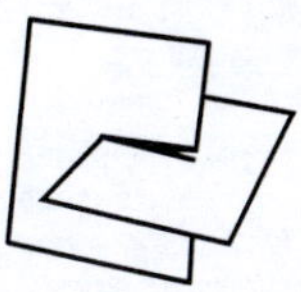

3. TAPE THE TWO PIECES.

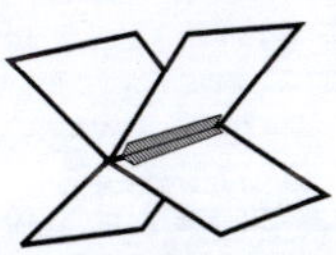

4. DRAW HALF A BUTTERFLY.

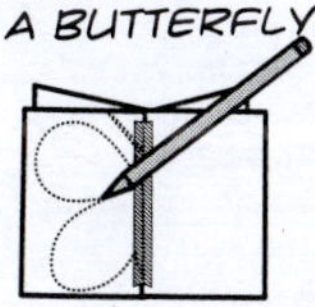

5. CUT TWO LAYERS TO MAKE A FULL BUTTERFLY.

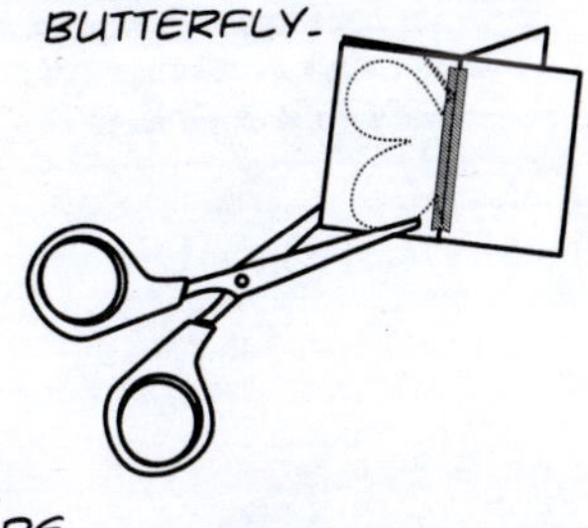

6. COLOUR THE BUTTERFLY.

7. MAKE 8 HOLES. WEAVE 2 THREADS AS SHOWN.

8. TIE THE ENDS.

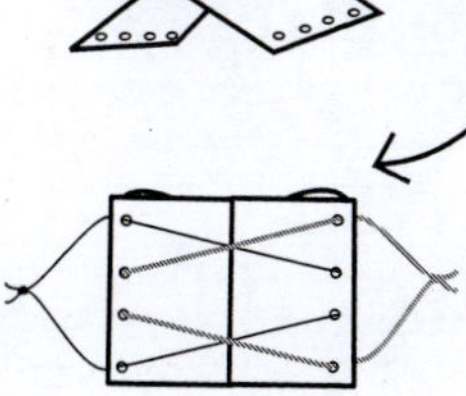

9. PULL AND RELEASE THE KNOTS TO MAKE THE BUTTERFLY FLAP ITS WINGS!

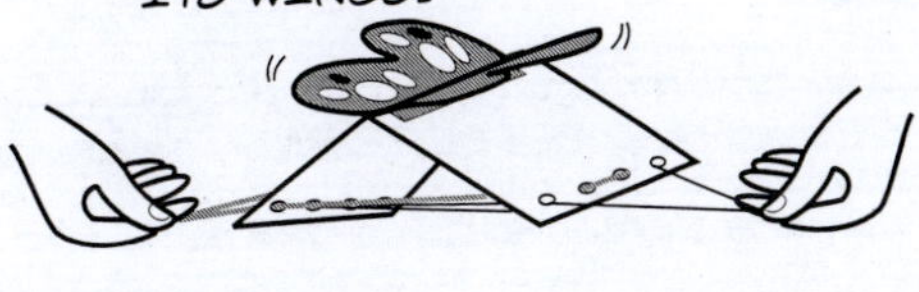

STRAW SCULPTURE

1 CUT THIN STRIPS AT THE TOP OF THE STRAW.

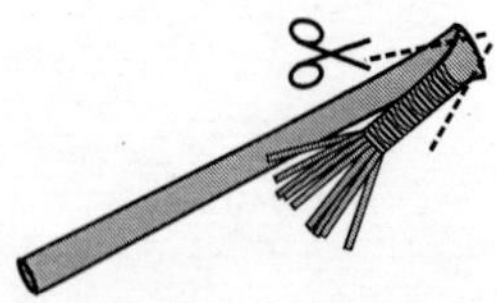

2 TO MAKE A DIAMOND PATTERN FOLD THE STRAW AND THEN NIP BOTH CORNERS AS SHOWN.

3 TO MAKE THE NEXT DIAMOND TURN THE STRAW BY 90 DEGREES. FOLD AND CUT AS BEFORE AND CONTINUE ...

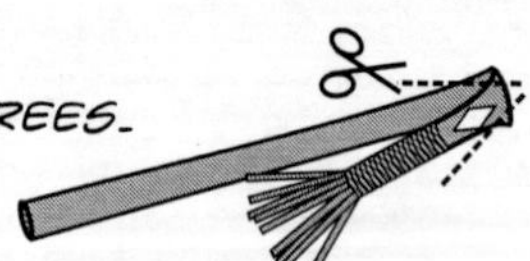

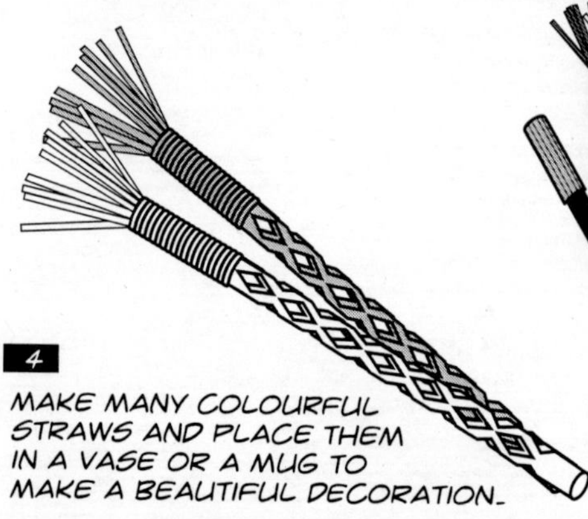

4

MAKE MANY COLOURFUL STRAWS AND PLACE THEM IN A VASE OR A MUG TO MAKE A BEAUTIFUL DECORATION.

ELEPHANT'S TRUNK

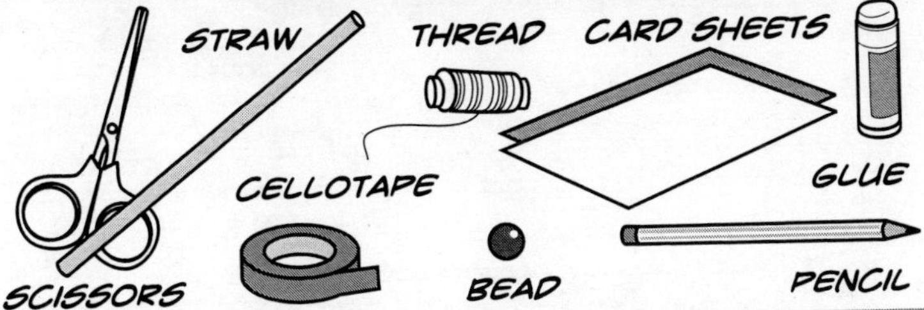

1 CUT A DIAMOND PATTERN ON THE STRAW.

2 FOLD A CARD SHEET AND DRAW AN ELEPHANT ON IT.

3 CUT ALONG THE LINES.

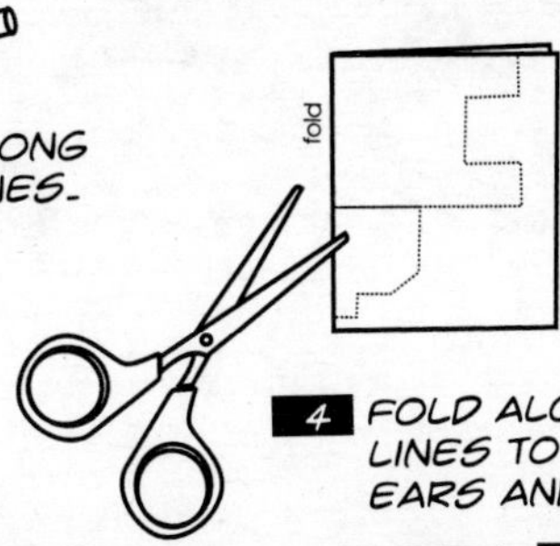

4 FOLD ALONG THE LINES TO MAKE EARS AND FEET.

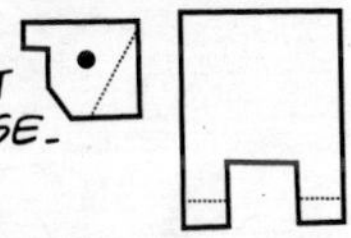

5 STICK THE FEET ON A CARD BASE.

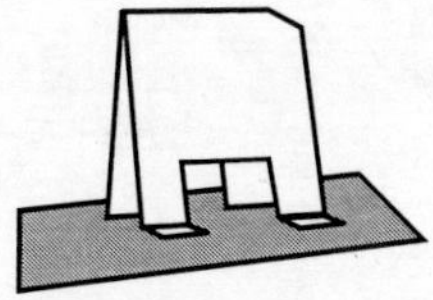

6 STICK THE STRAW AS SHOWN AND WEAVE A THREAD THROUGH IT.

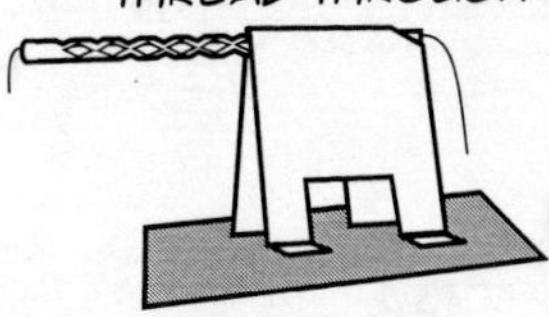

7 TAPE THE LEFT END OF THE THREAD TO THE STRAW. TIE A BEAD AT ONE END. STICK THE HEAD.

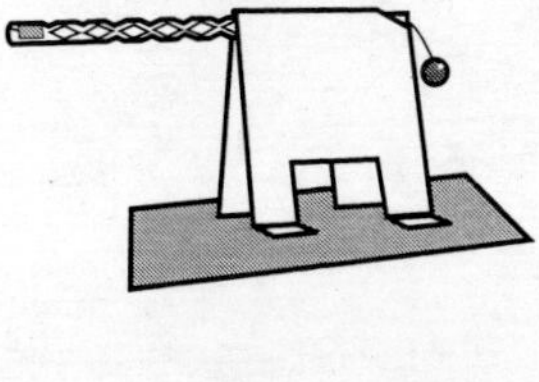

8 NOW PULL THE BEAD TO MAKE THE ELEPHANT LIFT ITS TRUNK!

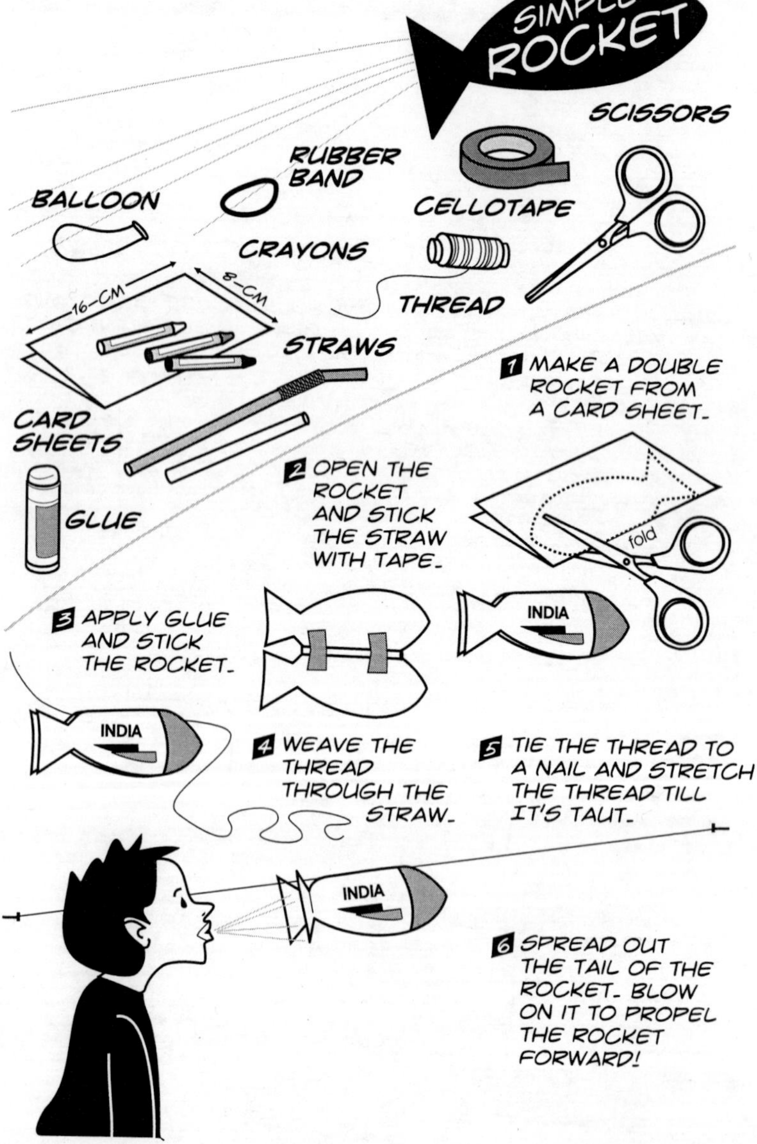
SIMPLE ROCKET
SCISSORS
RUBBER BAND
BALLOON
CELLOTAPE
CRAYONS
16–CM
8–CM
THREAD
STRAWS
CARD SHEETS
GLUE
1 MAKE A DOUBLE ROCKET FROM A CARD SHEET.
fold
2 OPEN THE ROCKET AND STICK THE STRAW WITH TAPE.
INDIA
3 APPLY GLUE AND STICK THE ROCKET.
INDIA
4 WEAVE THE THREAD THROUGH THE STRAW.
5 TIE THE THREAD TO A NAIL AND STRETCH THE THREAD TILL IT'S TAUT.
INDIA
6 SPREAD OUT THE TAIL OF THE ROCKET. BLOW ON IT TO PROPEL THE ROCKET FORWARD!

BALLOON ROCKET

1 MAKE A ROCKET AS SHOWN ON THE PREVIOUS PAGE.

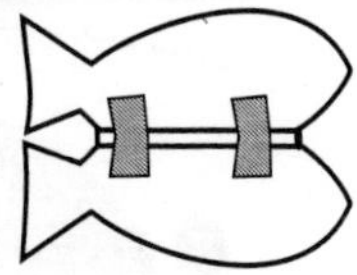

2 STICK A BENDY STRAW AS SHOWN.

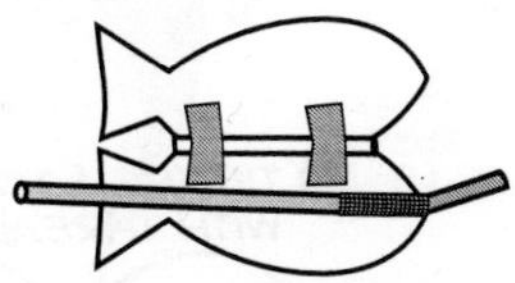

3 CLOSE AND STICK THE TWO HALVES OF THE ROCKET.

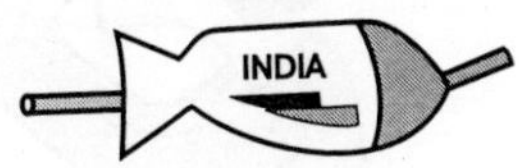

4 ATTACH A BALLOON TO THE BENDY STRAW WITH A RUBBER BAND.

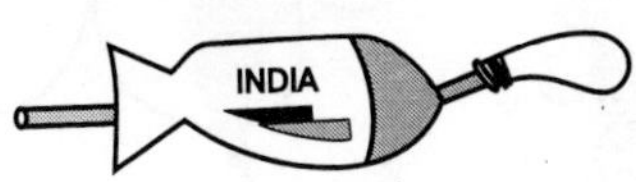

5 TIE A PIECE OF THREAD TO A NAIL AND STRETCH IT TILL IT'S TAUT. INFLATE THE BALLOON!

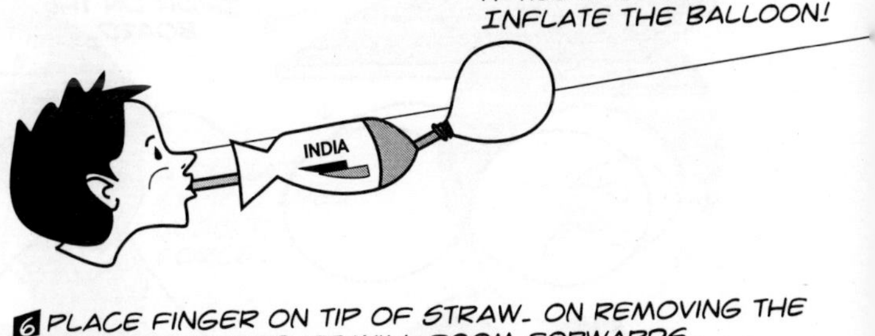

6 PLACE FINGER ON TIP OF STRAW. ON REMOVING THE FINGER THE ROCKET WILL ZOOM FORWARDS.....

FALLING SPIDER

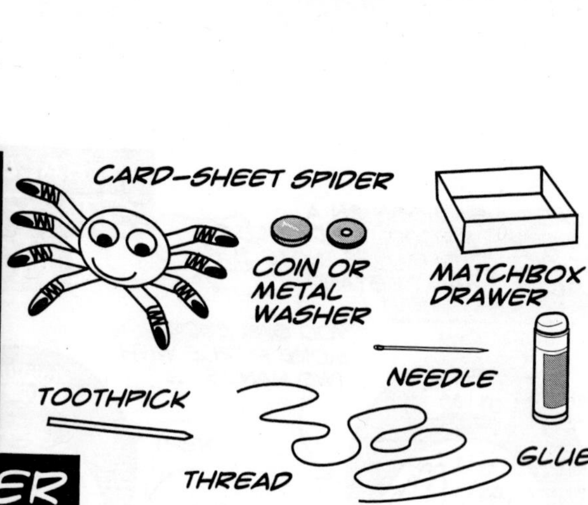

1. GLUE A COIN OR WASHER INSIDE A MATCHBOX DRAWER.

2. ATTACH A TOOTHPICK AS SHOWN.

3. WEAVE THREAD AS SHOWN. THE THREAD MUST RUB THE TOOTHPICK. TIE LOOPS AT BOTH ENDS.

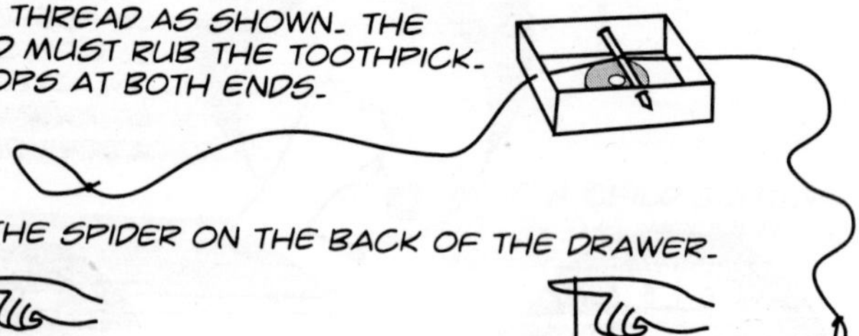

4. PASTE THE SPIDER ON THE BACK OF THE DRAWER.

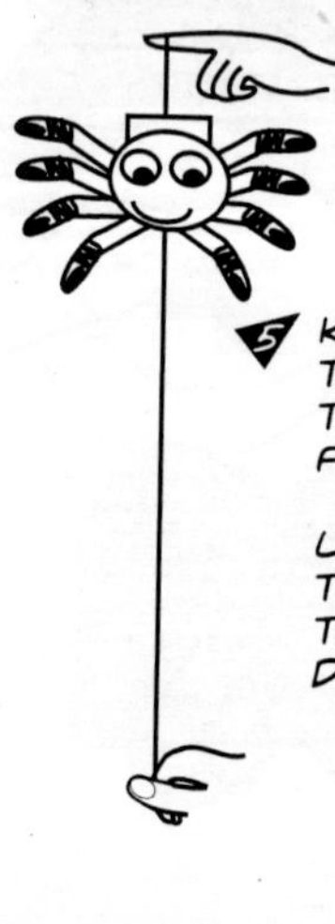

5. KEEP THE THREAD TIGHT TO STOP THE SPIDER FROM FALLING!

LOOSEN IT TO MAKE THE SPIDER DROP.

CRAWLING COIN

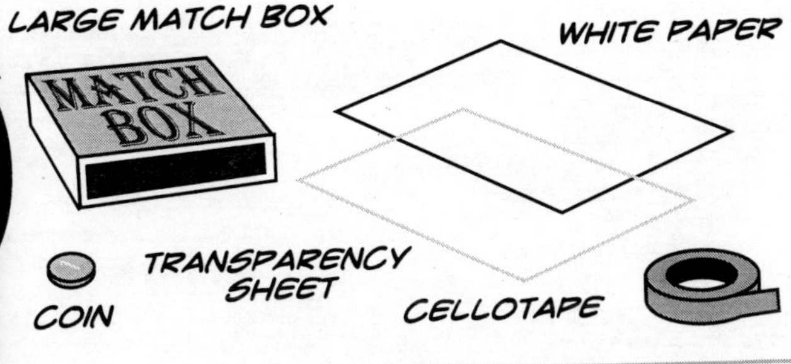

1. PASTE WHITE PAPER ON THE MATCHBOX.

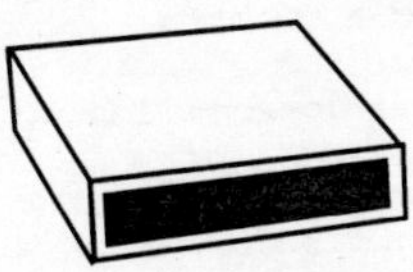

2. STICK THE TRANSPARENCY SHEET ON THE WHITE PAPER WITH CELLOTAPE.

3. SLIP A COIN BETWEEN THE PAPER AND THE TRANSPARENCY SHEET.

4. HOLD THE MATCHBOX VERTICALLY AND SUPPORT THE COIN WITH A FINGER.

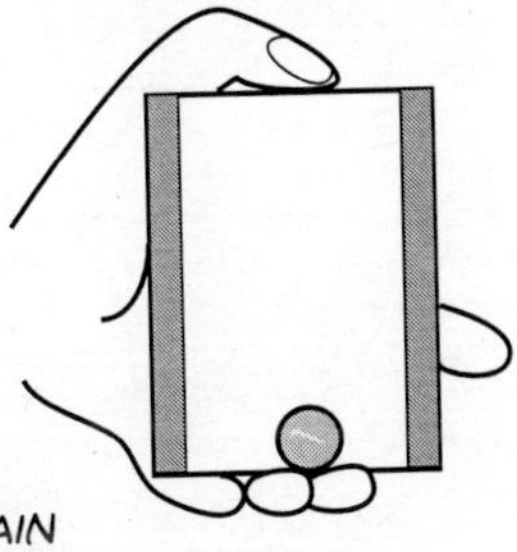

5. TAP HARD ON THE MATCHBOX.

PLUCK-STRING SPIN DISC

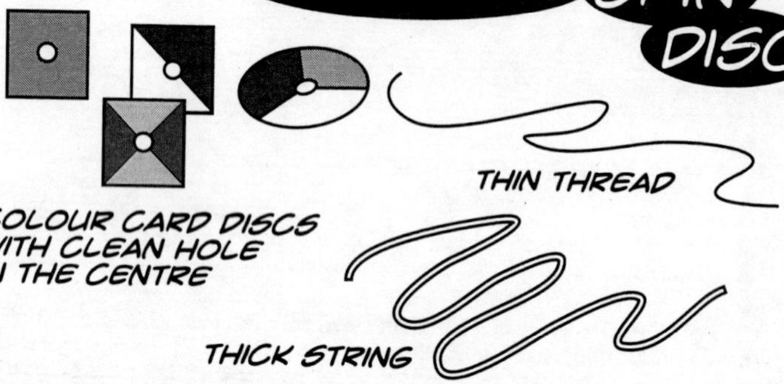

1. WEAVE THE STRING LOOSELY IN THROUGH A COLOUR DISC. TIE KNOTS AT BOTH ENDS.

2. HOLD THE STRING TIGHT.

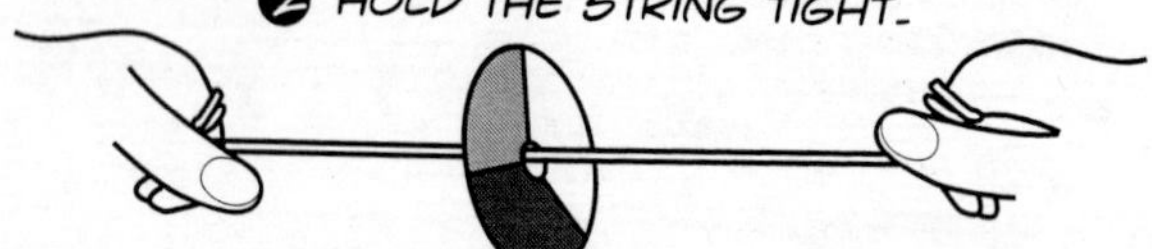

3. PLUCK THE STRING WITH YOUR THUMB.

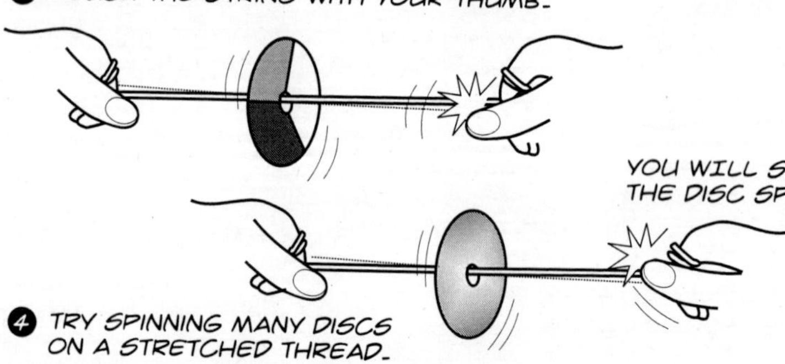

4. TRY SPINNING MANY DISCS ON A STRETCHED THREAD.

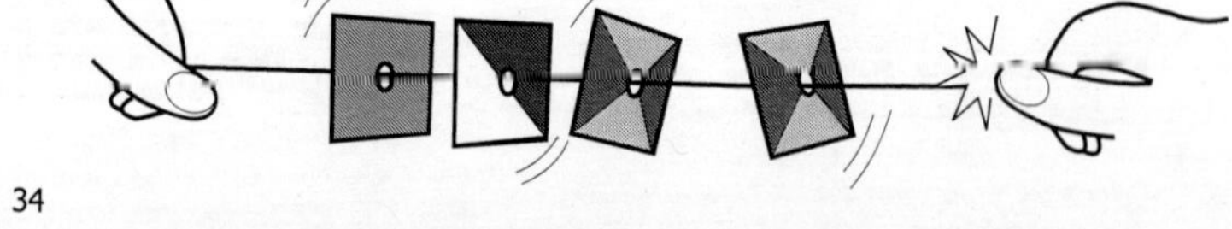

MOTHER TERESA'S MEDICINE POUCH

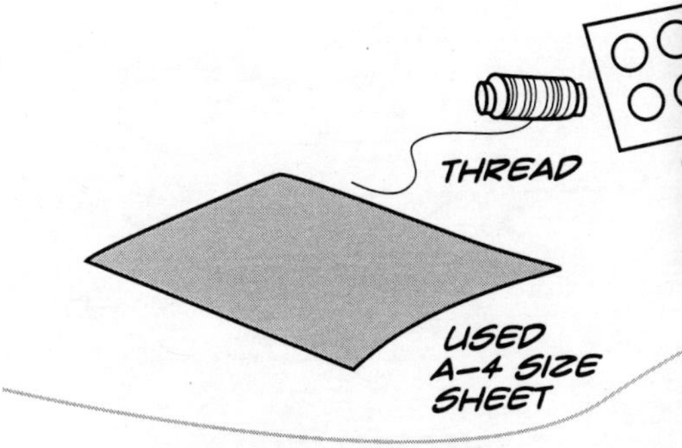

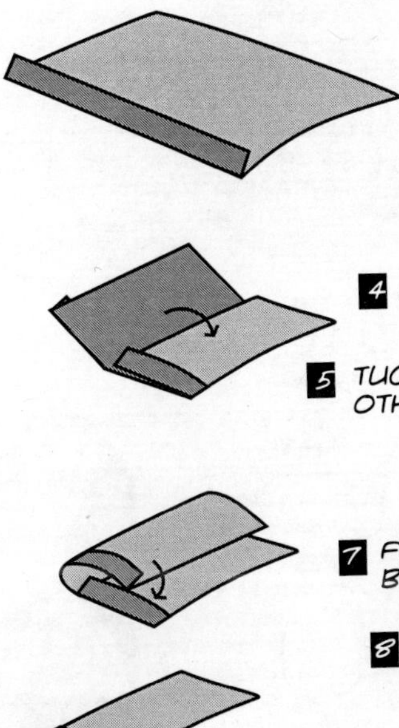

1. TAKE A USED A-4 SHEET.
2. FOLD A 3-CM EDGE ALL ALONG THE LENGTH.
3. TURN THE PAPER AROUND.
4. FOLD IT IN THREE EQUAL PARTS.
5. TUCK ONE FLAP INTO THE OTHER TO MAKE THEM LOCK.
6. TURN IT AROUND.
7. FOLD SKEWED TRIANGLES AT BOTH TOP CORNERS.
8. FOLD THE FLAP AND TUCK IT INTO THE POCKET. TIE A STRING TO THE POUCH.

FACE FRAUD

1. FILL THE BALLOON WITH WHEAT FLOUR.

2. PUSH WITH A PEN TO PACK MORE FLOUR.
3. TIE A KNOT.

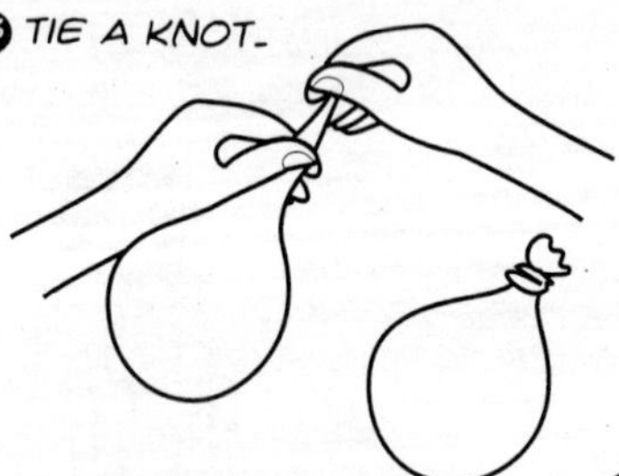

4. DRAW A FACE ON THE BALLOON.

5. SQUEEZE IT TO MAKE FUNNY FACES, THE WAY YOU WOULD DO WITH CLAY DOUGH.

BOYLE'S BALLOON

1. BLOW A BABY BALLOON.

2. TRIM THE EXTRA RUBBER.

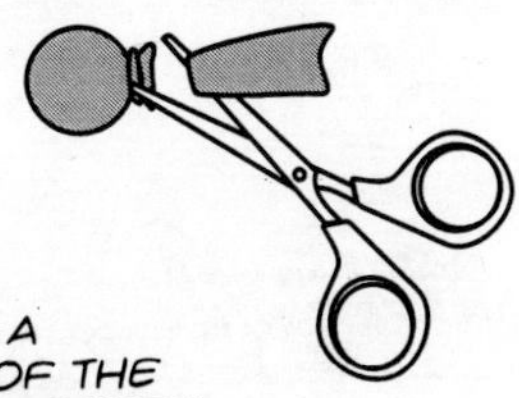

3. PLACE THIS BABY BALLOON INSIDE A SYRINGE BARREL. NOTE THE SIZE OF THE BALLOON BULB UNDER NORMAL PRESSURE.

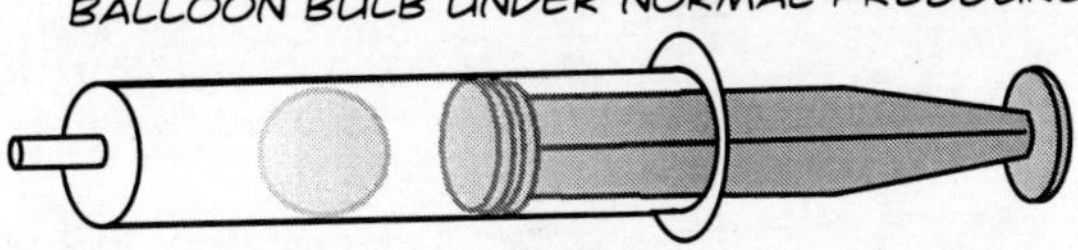

4. SHUT THE OUTLET OF THE SYRINGE WITH YOUR FINGERTIP AND PUSH THE PISTON IN. THE BABY BALLOON WILL SHRINK IN SIZE AS THE AIR PRESSURE INCREASES.

5. SLOWLY PULL OUT THE PISTON. WITH DECREASE IN AIR PRESSURE THE BALLOON WILL INCREASE IN SIZE!

BOTTLE TURBINE

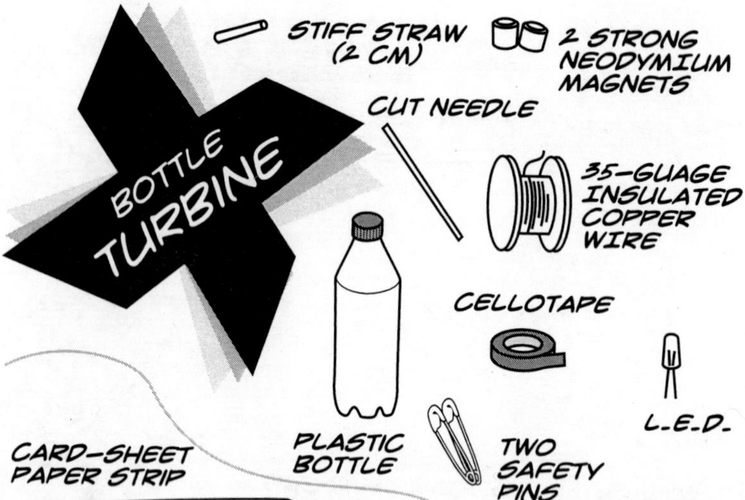

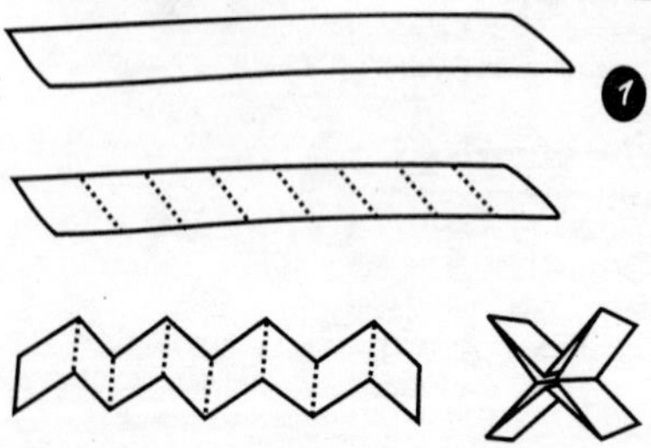

1. FANFOLD THE CARD STRIP AND STICK ITS ENDS TO MAKE AN X-SHAPED TURBINE.

2. MAKE AN OFF-CENTRE HOLE IN THE BOTTLE CAP. FIX A STIFF STRAW IN IT.

3. STICK A NEEDLE IN THE TURBINE. AFFIX TWO SAFETY PINS WITH TAPE ON THE CAP. PLACE THE NEEDLE AXLE IN THE PINHOLES.

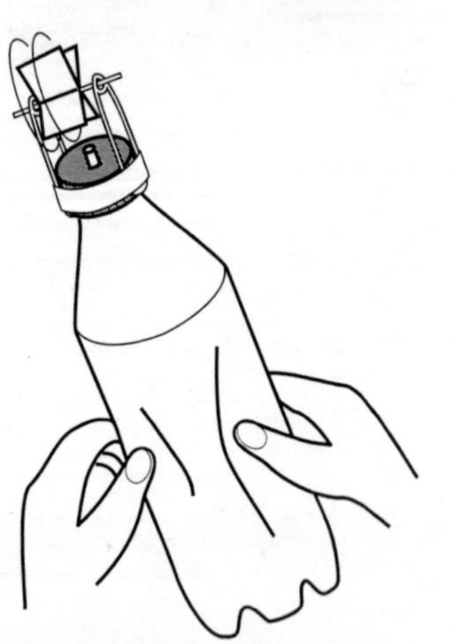

4. SCREW THE CAP ON BOTTLE. ON SQUEEZING AND RELEASING THE BOTTLE AN AIR-JET WILL TURN THE TURBINE.

5 NOW CUT THE BASE OF THE BOTTLE AND MOVE IT UP AND DOWN IN A JAR OF WATER. AIR EXPELLED FROM THE BOTTLE WILL CONTINOUSLY TURN THE TURBINE.

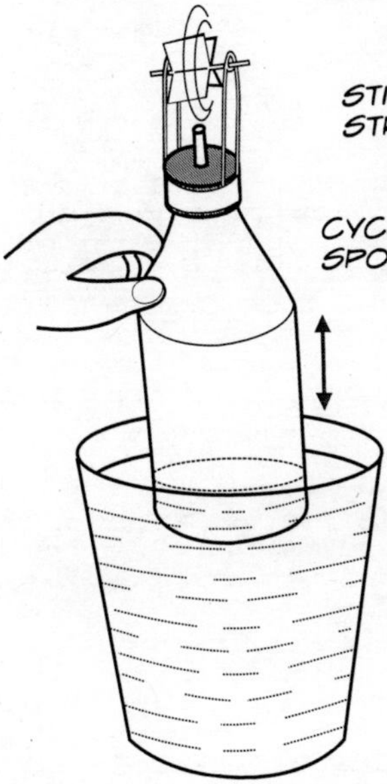

6 MAKE A **GENERATOR** UNIT USING TWO STRONG MAGNETS AND MOTOR-REWINDING WIRE.

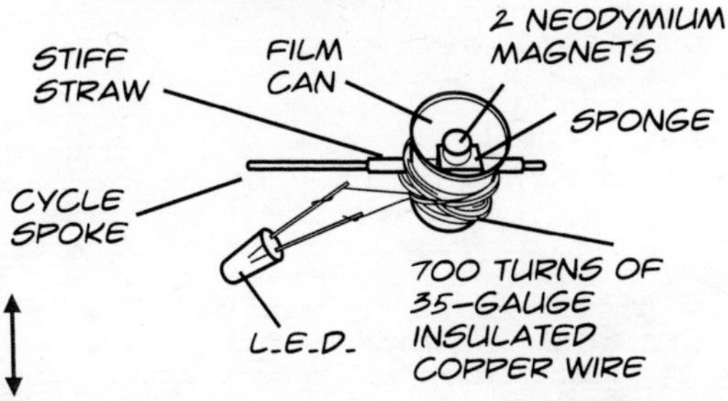

7 ATTACH A CARD-SHEET TURBINE TO THE GENERATOR.

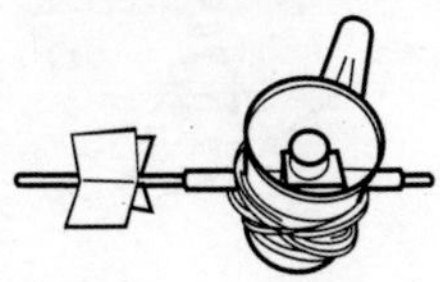

8 NOW MOVE THE CUT BOTTOM BOTTLE UPSIDE DOWN IN A JAR OF WATER. AS THE WATER ENTERS THE BOTTLE IT WILL EXPEL AIR.

THIS JET OF AIR WILL SPIN THE TURBINE, WHICH IN TURN WILL SPIN THE MAGNETS INSIDE THE COIL. THIS SPINNING MAGNETIC FIELD WILL INDUCE AN EMF IN THE COIL, WHICH WILL LIGHT THE L.E.D.

BOTTLE BAROMETER

1 MAKE A HALF-CUT ALONG AN AIRTIGHT PLASTIC BOTTLE.

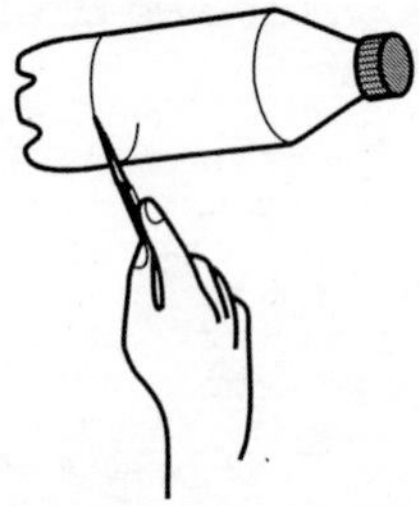

2 PRESS WITH YOUR THUMB TO MAKE A CONCAVE SHAPE.

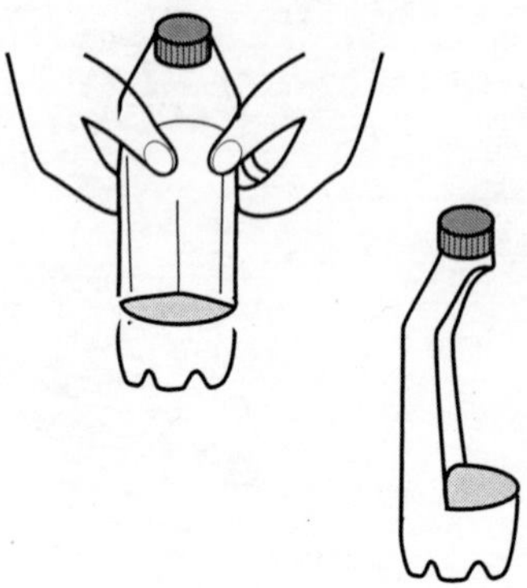

3 DIP THE BOTTLE IN A BUCKET TO FILL IT WITH WATER.

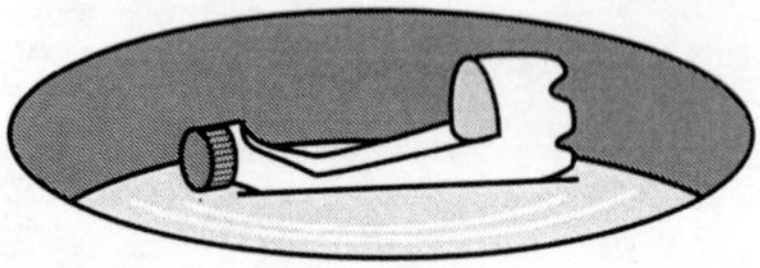

4 CHECK THE LEVEL OF WATER.

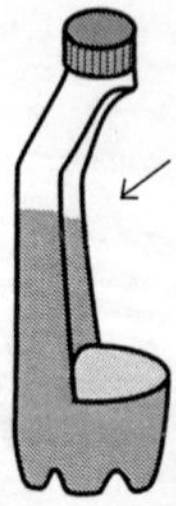

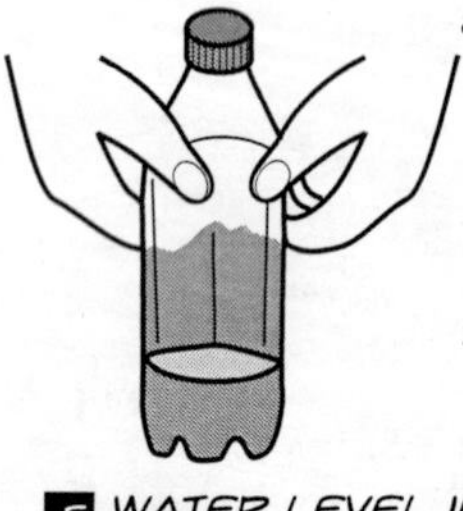

5 WATER LEVEL IN THE NARROW PART CAN BE CHANGED BY CHANGING THE VACUUM.

WHY DO YOU THINK THE WATER LEVEL RISES IN THE NARROW PART?

INERTIA BOTTLES
2 BOTTLES
GLOSSY PAPER STRIP
1 REMOVE THE CAPS FROM 2 BOTTLES. FILL THEM 3 QUARTERS WITH WATER.
2 PLACE A PAPER STRIP ON A BOTTLE'S MOUTH.
3 PLACE THE MOUTH OF THE OTHER BOTTLE ON TOP OF THE FIRST BOTTLE. YOU MAY LOSE SOME WATER.
4 STRIKE THE END OF THE STRIP HARD WITH ONE FINGER.
THE STRIP WILL FALL, BUT THE BOTTLES WILL STAND ONE ON TOP OF THE OTHER.

BOTTLE-LID SPINNER

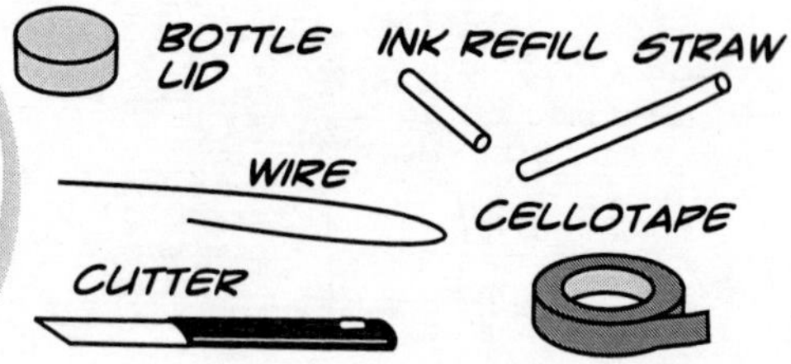

❶ CUT VANES IN THE BOTTLE LID.

❷ MAKE A HOLE IN THE BOTTLE LID AND FIX A PIECE OF AN INK REFILL AS A BEARING.

❸ MOUNT THE LID ON A WIRE AS SHOWN. THE WIRE LOOPS WILL PREVENT THE LID FROM FALLING.

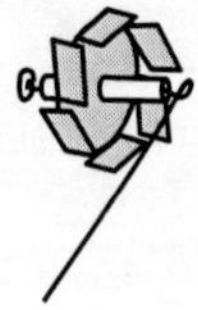

❹ FIX A 6-CM-LONG STRAW TO THE WIRE WITH TAPE.

❺ THEN BLOW THROUGH THE STRAW.

MARBLE TIPPY-TOP

4 MARBLES

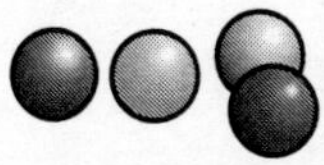

RUBBER GLUE (FEVIBOND)

1. STICK 3 MARBLES TOGETHER.

2. GLUE THE FOURTH MARBLE TO MAKE A TETRAHEDRON.

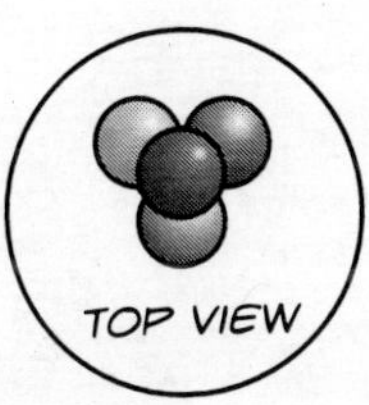

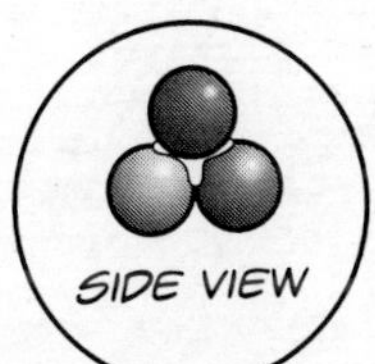

3. GRIP THE TOP MARBLE AND SPIN IT LIKE A TOP.

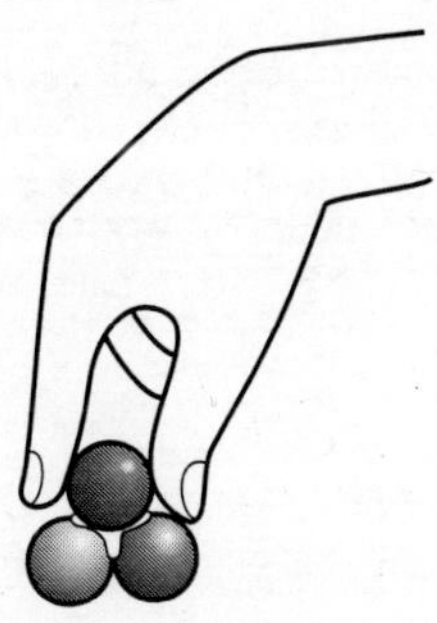

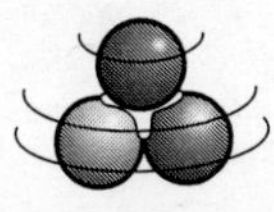

AFTER A WHILE YOUR TOP WILL UPTURN!

CIRCLE TO ELLIPSE

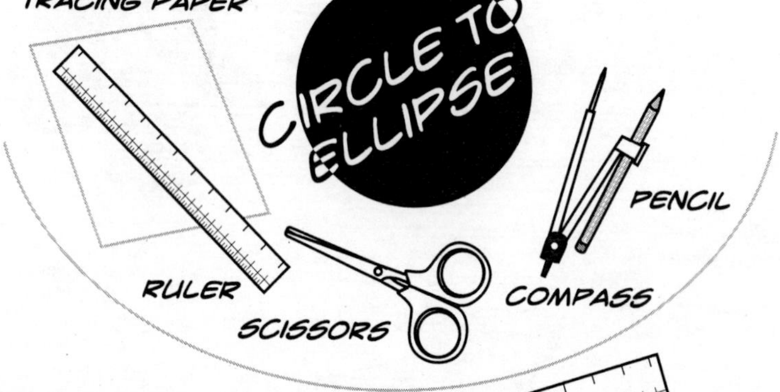

1. DRAW A 7-C- RADIUS CIRCLE ON A TRACING PAPER.
2. CUT OUT A CIRCLE.

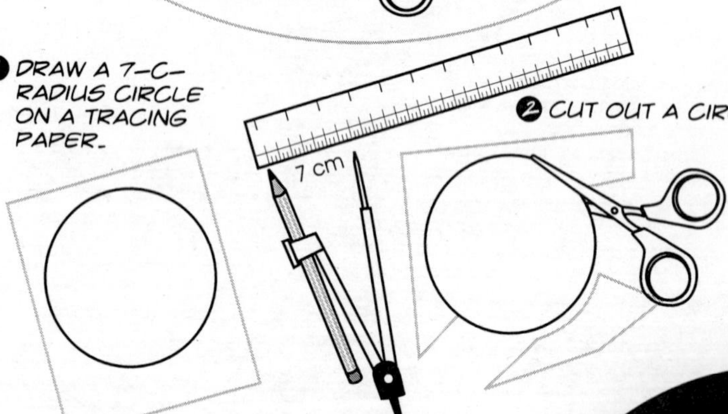

3. MARK CENTRE 'C' AND POINT 'X' ABOUT 2 CM FROM THE CENTRE.
4. FOLD A CHORD SO THAT THE EDGE OF THE CIRCLE FALLS ON 'X'.

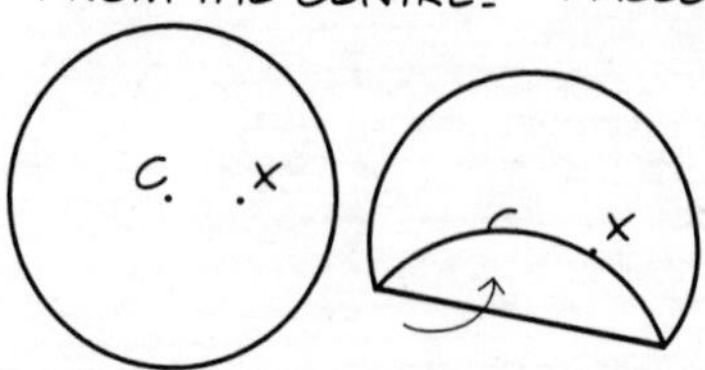

5. KEEP FOLDING. EACH TIME THE CIRCUMFERENCE MUST FALL ON POINT 'X'. SOON YOU WILL SEE AN ELLIPSE WITH 'C' AND 'X' AS ITS FOCI.

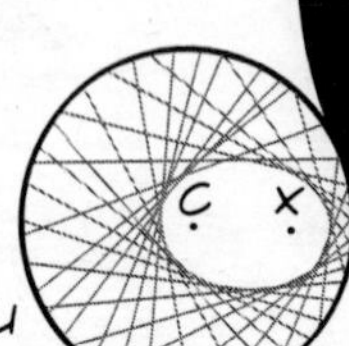

THE ELONGATION OF THE ELLIPSE DEPENDS ON HOW FAR 'X' IS FROM 'C'.

CLOSER WILL GIVE YOU A MORE ROUNDED AND FARTHER WILL GIVE YOU A MORE ELONGATED ELLIPSE.

BAG JACK

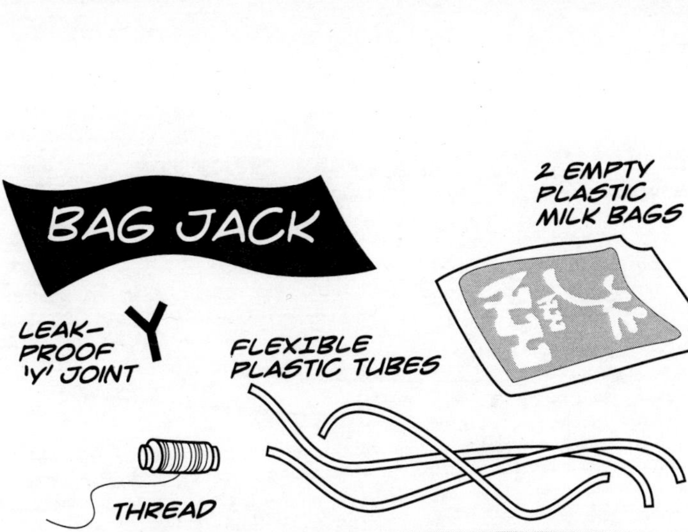

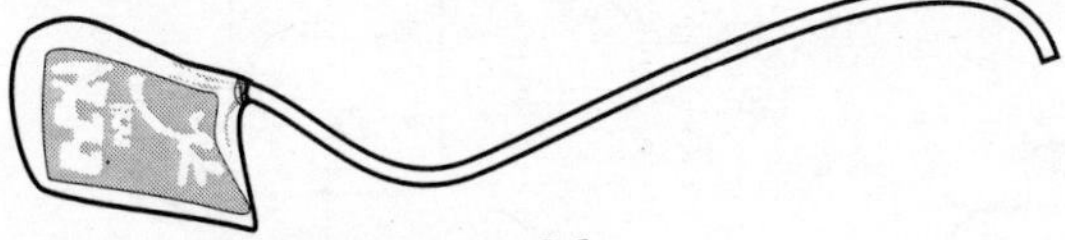

1. TIE TUBES TO 2 PLASTIC BAGS WITH STRONG THREAD.

2. ATTACH THE 'Y' JOINT AS SHOWN.

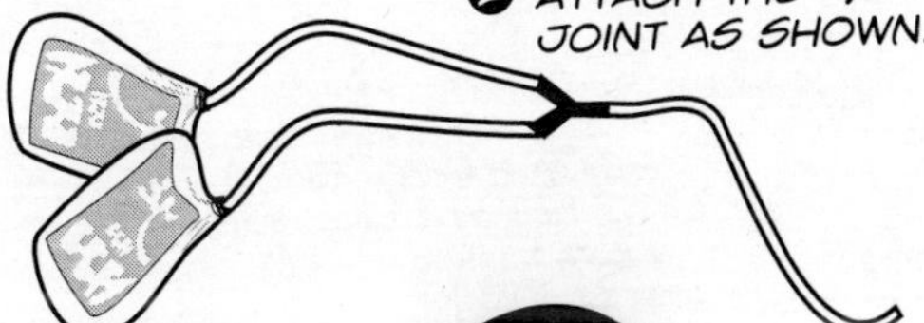

3. BLOW HARD, AND YOU SHOULD BE ABLE TO LIFT A 10-KG LOAD OF BOOKS!

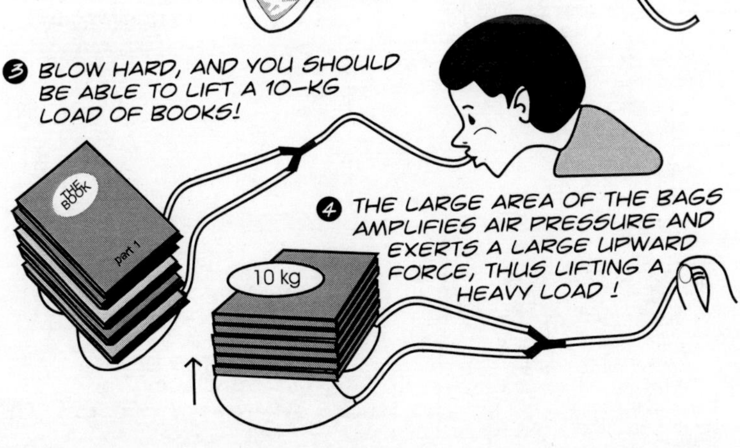

4. THE LARGE AREA OF THE BAGS AMPLIFIES AIR PRESSURE AND EXERTS A LARGE UPWARD FORCE, THUS LIFTING A HEAVY LOAD!

TOTAL INTERNAL REFLECTION

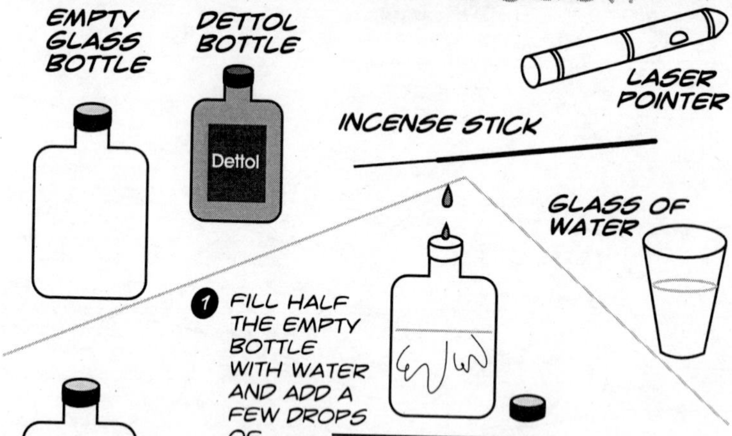

1. FILL HALF THE EMPTY BOTTLE WITH WATER AND ADD A FEW DROPS OF DETTOL.

2. POINT A LASER BEAM PARALLEL TO THE WATER LEVEL. THE BEAM WILL GO IN A STRAIGHT LINE.

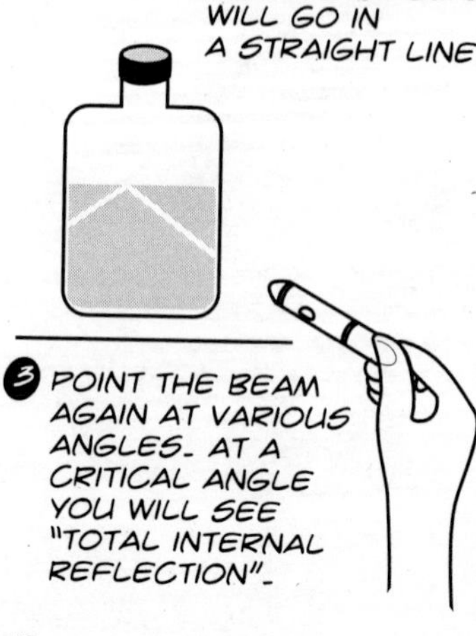

3. POINT THE BEAM AGAIN AT VARIOUS ANGLES. AT A CRITICAL ANGLE YOU WILL SEE "TOTAL INTERNAL REFLECTION".

4. FILL THE BOTTLE WITH SMOKE BY USING A BURNING INCENSE STICK. THEN PUT THE CAP ON.

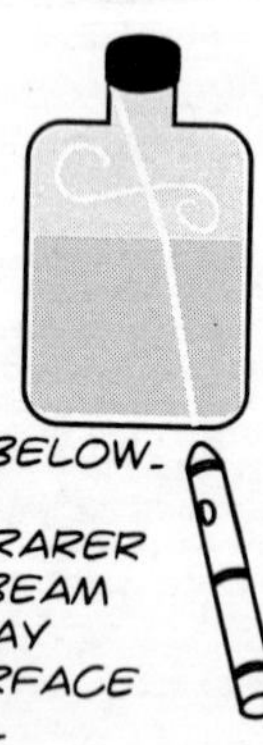

5. POINT THE LASER FROM BELOW. GOING FROM DENSER TO A RARER MEDIUM, THE BEAM WILL BEND AWAY FROM THE SURFACE OF THE LIQUID.

TETRA MEASURES

1 THIS TETRAPAK CONTAINED 200 ML OF FRUIT JUICE. CUT THE TOP TO MAKE A 200-ML MEASURE. CUT FURTHER TO MAKE 100-ML OR 50-ML VOLUME MEASURES. THESE SAFE AND WATERPROOF CUPS CAN BE FLATTENED AND STOWED AWAY IN ANY POCKET DURING TRAVEL.

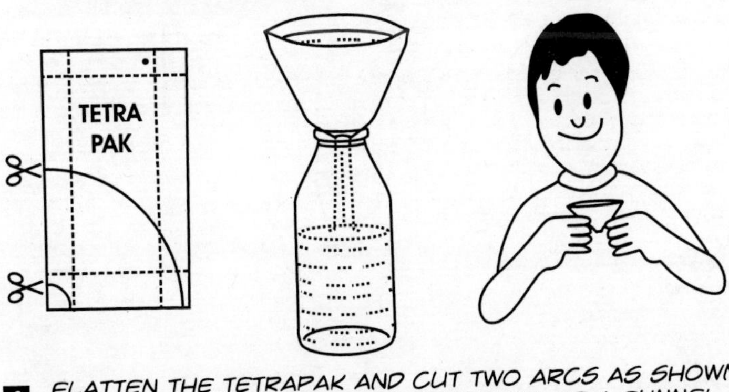

2 FLATTEN THE TETRAPAK AND CUT TWO ARCS AS SHOWN. OPEN THE CUT PORTION AND SHAPE IT LIKE A FUNNEL. THIS COLLAPSIBLE FUNNEL CAN BE FLATTENED AND CARRIED IN A POCKET TOO.

ANIMAL JIGSAW

1 DRAW 17 ANIMALS ON A THICK CARDBOARD OR PLYWOOD PIECE. THEN CUT THEM WITH A CRAFT KNIFE OR A FRET SAW. YOU CAN STAND THESE ANIMALS INDIVIDUALLY TO MAKE A ZOO OR EVEN JOIN THE PIECES INTO A JIGSAW.